Advance Praise for Kurt Cole Eidsvig's *Drowning Girl*

Kurt Cole Eidsvig's writing is noteworthy in how it synthesizes the aesthetics of pop art with street-level romantic minimalism, bound together in a worldview apprenticed at once to visual arts, poetry, fiction, and screenwriting. In *Drowning Girl*, Eidsvig dances through interconnected worlds—inner, outer, emotional, harsh at times, and, one feels, even joyful—to tell a story at once visceral and liminal, personal and yet deeply informed by the cultural moment. His prose-poem-novel seems to take "I don't care! I'd rather sink. . ." from Lichtenstein's *Drowning Girl* as a starting point, an invitation, and a microcosm. Eidsvig's work, centered at the intersection of art and life, is irrepressible, unique, entertaining, clever, and perhaps because of this, essential.

—Michael Davis, author of *Gravity*

Drowning Girl is a euphoric and melancholic meditation on existing between landscapes. How do you establish a YOU ARE HERE, when you are also there and there and there? This is the mind's travel itinerary, dizzying as Lichtenstein's canvas of Ben Day dots: Key West, the Berkshires, Boston, New York, Montana. How do you travel when the map is coming apart at its folds? When no landscape is drawn to scale? You orient yourself by building your own cathedrals: art, old neighborhoods, the memories of lovers, mothers, fathers, and friends. This is where you came from. This was the winding path you took. You can look back, even savor the footnotes, but you can't stay long. A seasoned traveler knows the arrows of time are pointed, annoyingly, forward. Eidsvig welcomes us to hitch a ride in order to find out how to curate a life when your museum is ever moving. This is a painstaking cataloging of the bitter and the beautiful moments in life. The reader is invited to be, like the narrator, a "painter in a hurricane"—storm chaser, survivor, then excavator, unearthing the artful from the numbing disaster of technology and pop culture.

—Wendy Erman Harvey, author of *Vicinity*

Drowning Girl is a tour de force of poetry that alludes, scampers, plays and generously appropriates from a wide variety of sources, using the Roy Lichtenstein painting as ekphrastic inspiration, unmasking the "Brad" in the painting as bard, lover and playmaker. Replete with art and literature references, this Ben-Day dotted work emits Morse codes filled with delight.

—Michel Steven Krug, author of *Jazz at the International Festival of Despair*

Eidsvig's *Drowning Girl* is an immersive and deeply evocative journey through art, addiction, obsession, and the enduring power of fleeting connection amidst the relentless tide of entropy. Cutting, profound, and at times laugh-out-loud funny, *Drowning Girl* is both a celebration of art and a testament to the unlikely convergence of grief and grace through which it is made manifest. It's a wonderful book.

—Aryn Kyle, author of *Boys and Girls Like You and Me*

DROWNING GIRL

Published by Unsolicited Press.
Printed in the United States of America.
First Edition.

 This is a work of fiction. Unless otherwise indicated, all the names, characters, businesses, places, events and incidents in this book are either the product of the author's imagination or used in a fictitious manner. Any resemblance to actual persons, living or dead, or actual events is purely coincidental.

Attention schools and businesses: for discounted copies on large orders, please contact the publisher directly.

For information contact:
Unsolicited Press
Portland, Oregon
www.unsolicitedpress.com
orders@unsolicitedpress.com
619-354-8005

Cover Design: Kathryn Gerhardt
Editor: S.R. Stewart

ISBN: 978-1-963115-10-9

DROWNING GIRL

Kurt Cole Eidsvig

PREFACE

One of the best parts about being a poet is lying. Speaking of lying, I had a friend in Boston who used to say, "Do you know how I know you are lying? Your lips are moving."

He felt like I had a penchant for bending the truth.

But in poetry, we call this lying *poetic license.* The idea is that by this non-accredited licensure, poets can somehow reveal more of the absolute truth about something by lying. It's basically all the fun of lying with none of the guilt.

Do you know how I know you are using poetic license?

Your fingers are typing. Your pen is scribbling. Your voice is recording. Your phone is texting. Your computer is emailing. Your postcards are mailing.

None of this sounds as good as what my buddy Billy from Boston said. All of it is true in the case of this book though. Not poetically true. Actually true. This is a book-length poem made up of multiple forms of writing.

Why?

To tell the story of the individual dots in a Roy Lichtenstein painting. Of course.

0 0 0

Do you know how I know you are using your poetic license? Your credit card is ordering Craigslist ads.

More non-poetic truths: At one point I hired people through Craigslist ads to go stand in front of the iconic Roy Lichtenstein painting *Drowning Girl*, then hung/hanging in an elevator bay at the Museum of Modern Art in New York City (MoMA). Their job was to count the dots in the painting.

Except I used poetic license when I hired them. I was lying. I didn't want them to count the dots, really. Or rather, I didn't care how many dots there were. What I really wanted was to get them to stand there long enough to have a deep personal experience with the painting and their surroundings.

It was like one of those psychiatric experiments where the actual experiment is in the waiting room, rather than in the lab. At least that's what I learned from an episode of the TV show *Community.*

I paid these art workers 50 bucks a piece. The payment part had zero poetic license in sight. You are absolutely unable to use poetic license to pay bills. I have tried.

0 0 0

Here's another fact I can share without having to show my pleather poetic license holder and time-worn poetic license:

When I just went back to click the link to the original Craigslist ad I posted, the landing page reads:

> There is nothing here
>
> No web page for this address
>
> 404 Error

So much for nothing ever dies on the internet.

0 0 0

When I assigned these hapless victims the mind-bending task of counting the dots in a Lichtenstein, what was I really looking to gain? I was in the middle of writing a long poem about the said painting and thought I could get them to write parts of it for me. Or maybe inspire me. Or give me things to collage.

I sent them this survey after they completed their counting exercise:

Dear Museum Visitor:

Thank you for visiting the MoMA and spending some time with Roy Lichtenstein's *Drowning Girl,* 1963. As discussed, your responses to the following questions may be used as information for a book currently underway. Please do not spend too long on any single question and please answer one before continuing on to read and respond to the next (no more than 30 minutes at most).

- Name:
- Date of your visit to MoMA:
- How many dots did you count in *Drowning Girl*?
- Describe your experience while counting the dots.
- Do the dots remind you of anything?
- Did you encounter other dot counters?
- What was your experience like with other museum visitors while viewing *Drowning Girl*?
- What was your experience like with *Drowning Girl*?
- Have you ever had the feeling of drowning? When and in what situation did this occur?
- Have you ever felt like the girl in the painting? Have you ever felt like Brad? Explain.

- Are you Brad or the woman today?

0 0 0

Feel free to try and count the dots and respond to the survey yourself. The sequel to this book could easily be titled *Drowning Girl II. More Drowning. Drowningest Girl.*

Forgive me. I was using my poetic license.

0 0 0

As this book suggests later on down the road, the idea for *Drowning Girl* (the book) came from Barnett Newman. Years ago, I wondered about widening the "zip lines" in a Barnett Newman and painting whatever it was that was in there.

Incidentally, don't be put off by the lofty artistic references in this preface or this book. They aren't meant to deter you from enjoying the ride. A quick Google search for "episode of Community where they do an experiment" will yield as much fun as "Barnett Newman paintings."

Back to lofty artists: I actually tried to paint the inside of a Newman many times. My advice would be to go look at a Barnett Newman instead. Look for a while. Have a deep personal experience with one. They will open up for you all on their own. No bum poets or painters are required.

Do it even if no one pays you 50 bucks for your trouble.

0 0 0

Back to the *Drowning Girl* experiment. If you do decide to take the survey, it will be a lot of fun. But it won't be as immersive as the conceptual art piece that sprung out of having people count dots as an experiment.

But like Barnett Newman, *Drowning Girl* never disappoints.

0 0 0

Some words of caution: Beware. After the counting experiment and the questions, nearly all of the survey participants had deep and intense feelings about drowning.

0 0 0

A footnote: What do I think about poems with footnotes? I stole that idea from Jack Spicer. In his book *The Heads of the Town Up To the Aether* (1960), every poem has an extended footnote. Many times, the footnote is more important than the poem.

My friend Billy knew I was a thief in my younger days. He'd say, You'd steal anything that wasn't nailed down. You'd steal a guy's wallet and then help him look for it.

Similar to poetic licenses, poets are also granted a guilt-free license to steal. It's called *appropriation.*

You would appropriate anything that wasn't nailed down.

0 0 0

In addition to the surveys, this book steals (appropriates) songs, TV shows, texts, conversations, and writing. When a writer is really worried about the validity of their appropriation license, they add a footnote.

It's like poetic diplomatic immunity. Or a Get Out Of Jail Free card in a game of Monopoly.

0 0 0

What is Roy Lichtenstein's *Drowning Girl*? Maybe a story, maybe an allegory, maybe a metaphor for the atoms and subatomic particles that make up every inch of matter surrounding us.

Maybe it's a simple image stolen (appropriated) from a comic book. Maybe it is a mirror.

Maybe it is everything.

You have to go look and find out for yourself. You can use Google to find it. But after you find it, go look at it in person. You will find more of yourself in the looking.

0 0 0

What is this *Drowning Girl*? Experimental art, poetry, autobiography, numbers, fiction, emails, text messages, Ekphrastic (I had to look it up), letters, postcards, art criticism, fable, essay, creative non-fiction, survey responses, imagery, literary criticism, collage, free association, artist's statement, love letter, love poem, weather report, Morse Code, travel diary...

Dot. Dot. Dot.

Drowning Girl (the book) is the individual story of all those individual dots and who we are and who we might be when we look at them.

0 0 0

I didn't actually look up Ekphrastic. I knew what it was.

You know how I know you are lying? You pretended you had to look up Ekphrastic.

0 0 0

Thank you to the dozens of people who supported the creation of this book. And thank you to Unsolicited Press for giving this artwork its very own elevator bay to hang in.

0 0 0

In Section 39 of this book-length poem, I mention George Clooney and Julia Roberts. They share a great scene in the movie *Ocean's 11* that goes like this:

> Julia: *You're a thief and a liar.*
> George: *I only lied about being a thief.*

Sincerely,

Kurt Cole Eidsvig
Key West, 2023

I DON'T CARE!

I'D RATHER SINK--

THAN CALL BRAD
FOR HELP!

1

Circle button pressed with thumb pad, Brad snapped
an obligatory photo of the YOU ARE HERE sign
(*Renaissance Inn, Midtown*) with his iPhone on the way out,
posted to one of his Instagram accounts, walked
short city blocks crosstown, and counted fan hearts
on the elevator ride to the top. 42

and white-haired at the temples, the soon-to-be burgeoning
dot enthusiast allowed visitor clumps to disperse,
their maniac eyes like retro Pac-Man mouths, devouring
viewpoints from the edges. He set about designing
a museum-looking
strategy for the MoMA that day. Deciding to dedicate

this trip to hallway art—the all too often passed-over
placements near restroom doors and cafés, escalator
landings and elevator exits—he played solitaire
"Pick Your Favorite," and couldn't help but notice the
difference with Angela now gone. Brad kept remembering the
way she turned the light on.

2

Making his case to her looming and luminous, large
and glowing blank spot
(or prepping notes for future email missives,
his latest genre bent), his initial vote: "The Jasper Johns
series[1] on the wall there by the benches," he said
in the ellipses of his mind. Hashtags, or hash marks,
as frantic searching; the evolution of artist on hands and knees in prayer or passing pleasure,
displeased with romance's treasures and personal
sexual urging, progressing from finger painting desperation to stylized abstraction, all held on the hinge
of a decisive split; before and after. In retrospect, all our spastic attentions to disaster—this flailing—distill to a
caricature of trauma, and those three
ghosts of present and future/past outlasted Brad's capacity for air.

3

Circle back to their dinner in The Berkshires a long week-plus
before, when Brad said, "I'm an alcoholic; I suffer from euphoric recall. I remember

---

[1] Jasper Johns, *Tantric Detail I, II & III* from 1980 & 1981.

all the good times. And forget the worst of my ills."

"Alcoholics aren't the only ones who do that," she said.

"Except in alcoholics, it kills them," he said.

4

After all of Jasper Johns's floor searching—digging up treasure,

Looking loose floorboards through—the pictures flipped up and hanged or hanging

on walls depict an artist's hands longing for what's behind. Three paintings in an outside-the-café display show the arc of

American Art, a pivotal point

of autobiography. But walk back around the corner, like Brad did that Friday

at the end of September, and see your way to elevator doors again—the elevator

across from *Drowning Girl*—and you'll find

the single most important curatorial decision of any museum in the world.

A woman in the river, at first obscured by tourists taking selfies, reflecting

an elevator perfectly; taking everyone up and down.

5

Brad never considered Lichtenstein dots as rolling lettuce heads

before his long trip to the Northeast, but there they were in an email he'd sent

to Angela a week before. YOU ARE HERE he heard the elevator sign say

(*MoMA, NYC*).

One thing Brad felt sure of; he kept confusing departure and

arrival signs. He'd traveled up from Key West (the last spot on the map) in his mind,

to Miami; pushed through train station stops, commuter rail map marks,

and bus terminal delays—each stay rendered in colored filled-in circle-spots—before borrowing his mother's car for a road trip to visit Angela in her new surroundings that Tuesday.

6

If light could bother

in its ability to travel in streams

and photon particles too,

Drowning Girl conveyed the same.

The last time they'd met inside the National Gallery

in DC, he hadn't been comparably changed.

The last time he and Angela met,

at a lunch spot in Missoula, Brad hadn't wished
she'd flicked the light on and off in Morse Code,[2]
spelling letters in a row of abstract sculpture
to form the word STAY, before he shifted the car
into drive and accelerated away, slow.

7

Look at Lichtenstein dots for long enough
and you're bound to count. You're bound
to count up; you're bound to count down;
3, 4, 1.

3 = ···
4 = ····
1 = ·

---

[2] For more on the invention of Morse code, and the albatross of language Boston (represent) artist Samuel Morse hanged/hung around his neck with this invention, please see *The Greater Journey: Americans in Paris* by David McCullough (Simon & Schuster, 2011). Given all those dots from a practicing artist is there any question that Morse deserves a branch in the family tree with Seurat as one of Lichtenstein's granddaddies?

But after their dinner in The Berkshires,
    Brad kept wishing she (··· ···· ·)
    had asked him to stay (··· – ·– –·––).

    Even Roy Lichtenstein
    kept on this duplication,
    in cathedrals made of spots,

Brad had been hit with arrow points[3] and didn't know
    where to turn to safety and just sit down. Behind him,
    elevator doors yawned.

8

If alcohol could be both a stimulant and depressant,
explaining Brad's pre-sobriety tirades

---

[3] See Jasper Johns *Target With Plastic Casts,* 1955, an assemblage made in part by exploding Frank O'Hara's parts. Every artwork since might aspire to do the same. There's reasonable evidence Alfred Barr couldn't pull the trigger on buying this piece during Jasper's first show (a sellout, as was Lichtenstein's) because of Frank O'Hara's penis stuck behind a door (see *Figuring Jasper Johns,* by Fred Orton, (Reaktion Books, 2004). Instead, the MoMA owns "Target With Four Faces" from 1955, hanging and hung right down the corridor from Brad's eyes. Alfred Barr, possible CIA operative, quite literally asked Jasper Johns to keep his dick in the closet. See Keith Haring's *National Coming Out Day,* 1988, for the opposite of this (opposite in terms of clarity as well as doors opening).

turned to fistfights, excited shouts, and dance moves,

as clearly as his 3 AM photo album sullen flipbook fits

of tears and melancholy with Jimmy Buffett songs,
rivers could be both drops and streams.

No matter where you were. You were here.

9

At Higgs Beach in Key West three weeks later, Brad looked above at the clouds. They covered

up the spot of sun in the unmistakable shape

of a giant's foot.

10

All of this takes place [BACKSTORY]

in a time [BACKSTORY] severed by the dividing line

[UPRIVER BACKSTORY]

of summer into fall, three weeks stretched out to grasping

with a long train trip, a painter[4] occupied by an entire
coast, and a series of elevator rides [UPSTORY/DOWNSTORY].

---

[4] Read "Why I Am Not A Painter," by St. Francis O'Hara, The Patron Saint of New York and reincarnated Orpheus.

Facebook messages, Hurricane Matthew updates, coffee dates,
emails, texts, beach talks, and a spiritual retreat built up beneath seats of transports [TIME MACHINES].
Built to sound and faded.[5] Time: 21st Century, Earth.

11

Recently, a high-elevation airplane pilot who had edged up
beyond his flight path and seen the curve—*The Face of God*—explained things in formation. We were on folding chairs on the ground
and everyone clapped. "Don't worry, kid"
Pat Thorne used to say. "This is the only place on Earth

you can get up in front of a room, tell everybody
how you got arrested, stole from your family,
and generally screwed up your entire life
and still get a standing ovation."

---

[5] See the Doppler Effect. See Hubble Shifts. See red, see blue. Depending on where you are, color is everything (see Vonnegut in *Breakfast of Champions*). As an adjunct, peer into the Kepler Effect as well. What are you orbiting and what color do you announce in siren tones as you arrive? What about when you depart? Brad looked at the number flashes making up the elevator sign.

12

Outside the elevator exit on MoMA's top floor, before he even

made out his own name being exclaimed in the Lichtenstein balloon, Brad

caught his reflection in glass frame, his figure bouncing back in vivid black. What else could he do but take a self-portrait in the sheen? [SELFIE CLICK]

He thought of Jasper Johns pushing and groping for something there behind the wall. In the mirror of art in

hallways—the number plates made in individual LED light displays—the silver wall providing

background cracked and then PINGED, and yawned.

Whenever Brad looked deep at that level of black, he thought

of Rothko, and everything Rothko saw back there in

forever.

··· = S

···· = H

· = E

Brad's eyes kept scanning

Drowning Girl. She

was there with him.[6]

··· = S

···· = H

· = E

13

She.

She.

She.

She was the sky.

One, Two, Three

he counted.

She was the sky.

She was the sky full of targets.

Sky full of arrowheads.

Sky full of whales, white.

---

[6] The day Brad first thought of Samuel Morse and a Lichtenstein painting screaming Morse Code, whispering Morse Code, spelling out Morse Code, singing Morse Code to the audience of his dilated pupil eyes, he received his first paid response questionnaire to *The Drowning Girl Project.* Alexandria Woodson who visited the museum on 10/12/2016 claimed she counted over 100,000 dots in the painting. She said, "It was strenuous" and that she found herself becoming so engrossed in the task, "They reminded me of Morse code," she said.

Night sky full of snowflakes
falling down to ground on the top
of Mount Greylock before and after
burn scars changed the mountain's
history.

Sky full of harpoon holes.
Sky full of blowhole blacks.

Sky full of eyes stretched out
and blinking; twinkling pupils,
glittering and staring back.

Sky full of skin pores, hair follicles.
Sky full of wishes.
Sky full of horoscopes and premonitions.
Sky full of silver fountain coins.

Sky full of lily pads, of Seurat dots, of molecules,
and music notes.
Sky full of bubbles in glasses
of non-alcoholic champagne.

Sky full of bricks stacking up in infinite

cathedrals.

Below the dark mass, he waited in the idling.

From somewhere deep within
the darkened house she must have switched, turned
on, the porchlight.

Sky full of porchlight.

14

After leaving her, he'd written. Angela on her way
to an intellectual's foodie getaway
where she'd been charged with curating organic and exotic
vegetable displays for eating. Lichtenstein atoms

as lettuce in the bowling alleys of his mind, aimed
at various pins before he even arrived at MoMA.
Angela selecting lettuce; Brad
curating emails in his sent folder, wondering at time.

15

He wrote:

Somewhere in The Berkshires, a beautiful woman whose eyes literally sparkle

with mischief or knowing at times (who knew this happened in places besides

books?) stands in the produce section of a time machine and rolls heads of iceberg

lettuce across the dull tile. Because these vegetables are the most advanced

technology between here and the parking lot, they are spheres defined. They do

little skittering or bouncing but travel perfectly and true amongst the non-organic

fruits and careen off end-cap displays in unruly Dairy, Meat, and Grab & Go settlings.

The store, a memory of the 60s or 70s, a memory of cigarettes and hair curlers—

color palettes Kodak pre-ordered for the world—hasn't kept up with camera

technology or contemporary design, so the security guards do not descend

as pin setters in this opening scene for a bowling film.

This is an email, not a Coen Brothers movie.

This is an email that just appropriated

the set from a *Mad Men* episode where Betty Draper goes grocery shopping.

I'm sure I've asked if you ever watched the one where Don Draper reads O'Hara.[7]

How am I fortunate enough to know you?

16

A group of Japanese schoolgirls took turns
photographing each other next to the painting
while mimicking the *Drowning Girl's* hand position
and facial expression, too.[8]

17

From a pair of emails Brad spelled out in fingertip trips
across his smartphone screen:

[SUBJECT: CIRCLES INSTEAD]

Circle button.
Circle radio dial.

---

[7] See *Mad Men,* Season 2, Episode 1 "For Those Who Think Young," which features an excerpt from "Mayakovsky."

[8] From Claudia Eve Beauchesne's response to *The Drowning Girl Project*, October 15, 2016.

Circle tires.
Circle glass.
Circle back around.

[SUBJECT: EMAILS TO MYSELF IN MOMA]

These Johns pieces show a man clawing,

pushing, pressing to the other side; expression lines dying in time.

Around the corner, a Lichtenstein reflects a silver elevator opening and closing. Are paintings cathedrals or elevators? Is there ever

even a difference?

Jasper Johns: dash dash dash
Lichtenstein: dot dot dot

18

Brad used Google as memory (instead of prayer)

and searched his Gmail for some trace of his most recent meeting

with the girl with jet black reflectable hair; hair
the color of new highways, hair the color of night sky, hair
darker than Rothko dreams and nightmares.
There she was up there, sitting atop an exhibition critique

he'd written four years before (memory and prayer).
The only question on his mind now (and then) was what song
Lichtenstein had been tuning to
with his radio knob, circle notes streaming out
the windows, on the infamous ride to New York City.

19

Brad had written:
Conjuring the familiar folktale of a thirty-eight-year-old Roy Lichtenstein
heading over the bridge to Manhattan
with five canvases strapped to the top of his station wagon

sometime in 1961 is nearly impossible
amid the sprawling
grandeur of Washington, D.C., and the opulence of the National Gallery
of Art, host to the most recent leg of the artist's touring retrospective.

But we owe it to him to try, as comprehending the
weight of his contribution to the larger ideas of 20th Century
Art requires a trip back to the world of pre-Lichtenstein. Besides, what singular
lesson about art and life did this preeminent Pop artist teach us,

if not the permeating importance of context?

Take his most iconic works, for example, those like *Drowning Girl* from 1963. These paintings

rely on appropriation—a universal

understanding of their pedigree—in order to operate beyond decoration

as they enter the realm of masterpiece.[9]

So the last time they met, Brad and the *Drowning Girl*

had been in Washington D.C., and Brad, Brad

had been less than moved. He'd gone upstairs to Barnett Newman's *Stations*

of the Cross and had the appropriate

spiritual experience instead.

20

But he'd left the retrospective disenchanted.

He didn't know Roy any better

than he had months earlier at Boston's MFA.

Landscape painting as art curating, proving a precedent

---

[9] From *Big Red & Shiny*, December 16, 2012, with Brad writing under the pseudonym [REDACTED].

for rivers and arrow strikes.

Next, he'd left the NGA and walked across the street
to Ai WeiWei.
He'd sent Angela an email four some odd years ago, told her
to exit and do the same,
This showed you could know something and someone forever
in different cities and still get struck. The Berkshires
weren't the only arrow factory in America.

Outside, in the gleam of Skyscraper National Park, arrows as
building steeples drew dots up in the sky. Arrows
as clock hands
mocked the stillness of mailbox time.

21

He'd continued his post-Berkshires email to Angela:

If I were a fiction writer, there would be reasons.
The woman would be angry. She'd be rolling lettuce
at imaginary heads of people, not just other lettuce
heads.

She'd be muttering about lovers who were too beautiful

or ugly, people ugly inside but beautiful enough to be distrusted or pitied or both. She'd be counting things that don't matter or do.

(3,4,1;3,4,1;3), she'd be practicing her 1-10 split pickup
with pins of summer squash.

If I were a writer of fiction, I'd research bowling now. But I don't need research to know there's no such thing as a 1-10 split in bowling.

Every ancient store in The Berkshires is a time machine: Price Chopper, Big Y.

A 1-10 split is a dating term for when a pathetic person breaks up with a Sparkler.

Sparkler: a word Kathy Murgatroid used to describe Bennett before they dated. She knew he would be hers.

The woman is rolling lettuce. Not because she's resentful or insane.

Wouldn't rolling lettuce signal joy and clarity? It would to me. I've never seen you look so happy, or free.

The Berkshires are a time machine.

22

Here is something my mind whittled away at, came up with—bobbed

to surface—Wednesday morning:

When you talk about the chance of having time to curate shows, without

constraints or distractions, I am sure at your core, this is because

you would like to hone your craft and attention to show the world

how amazing painting can be.

When most people (including maybe me) think about focusing their craft

(in this case, art), they are

thinking at their core:

I would like to show people how amazing

I can be at painting.

This distinction is hugely important and signals an

incredible amount

of grace and humility and care. I would guess it is present in 1/10 of 1% of the population. Or, 1 in 10,000. 1 in 100,000?

It is something I didn't know about you but now do. I respect or admire it,

so much I could explode.[10]

Thus, there are men who broke with you who were victims of a 1-10,000 split.

23

When Brad was in High School, he hung[11] comic books in

plastic sleeves thumbtacked to the wallboards in his walk-in closet so hard he pressed

red circles against his fingertips and thumb, insisting they stick and STAY.

Despite the antiques and linen napkins, and all that closet space,

---

[10] [I could explode into a sky of snowflakes;

a sky scarred by confetti colors; a river

of magma capturing amber specs—like golden

stars—of forlorn and scattered volcanic ash]

[11] See "hanged."

they were by no means rich on the inside. Vodka—plastic gallon bottle vodka—

consumed child support and wages and sizable loans from Helen[12] and Red.

They ate bright orange welfare cheese

and second-hands from the Hostess Store. Hand-me-downs from brothers[13] Brad didn't have

became major staples of his wardrobe.

But in closet cathedrals to varying distances connected

electrically—and the musical tones of fingertips, lips, and tethered hearts—he hanged

Wolverine and *Batman*; *X-Men* odysseys and epic journeys

on closet walls.

He closed the door, lay on the floor, and spoke to his father

---

[12] Helen, the grandmom whose life Brad already wondered at. She lived to be 103.

[13] Brad wore hand-me-downs in plastic garbage bags from the Swillz brothers, a couple guys he never met. Years later, after he worked with Mike Swillz at Camp Bornebay, they moved in together with his brother Jed, a semi-professional soccer player and former captain of the Bay State Soccer Team. A TV commentator once called the sweeper "Stop Sign Swillz," and "Stoppey" or "Stop Sign" had stuck ever since. When they went to the gym together, Jed encouraged Brad to do pull-ups, and literally lifted him up and down off the ground when he could not. Brad's mother said, "Those are the boys who gave you clothes when you were growing up."

every Sunday night,

8 pm sharp, Eastern Time.

Brad spoke to girls and then their girlfriends.
He destroyed friendships with his voice, strong
Boston accent carving purposely misquoted excerpts from Robert B. Parker
books he'd studied to understand order and chaos[14] and the epigraphs
of the great John Donne.[15]

---

[14] If you ever get caught on the meaning of an Impressionist Landscape try out the imposition of order onto nature's chaos. The thing is, before the Atomic Bomb, believing in the rigor and righteousness of man in beating back the unruly darkness of instinctive death came easy. Now, see the cement walkways, or a footpath, architecture sprouting out from behind some crooked trees and the inhalant you breathe is dread. Your exhales fill with virus. We are the disease.

[15] John Donne might still be the best poet who ever lived. Last night in thinking of Angela and wondering at the mailbox, Brad Google-searched her some. He read against her exhibition catalogue essays, smiling photos too. At the start she looks like a girl who listens to Buffalo Tom in Cambridge whenever they're in town, and now there are the chamber sounds. Brad's world was disparate comic book collages hung/hanged in a metaphor for his brightly colored and heavily outlined heart. Her world is a blend of things making larger music. There were phones behind closet doors then, that now reside in minds. Angela makes art critical poetry with Poussinist lines. Brad made stabs at magazine shards. See above.

24

Less than two weeks from the day[16] Brad decided he wanted to tell her everything—

not as a confession, as he had nothing to confess besides the comfortably

uncomfortable connection between them—but as an involuntary reaction

to arrows shot in rainbow arcs, she asked if he was safe from hurricane's path.

Angela hadn't looked up to the end of the Florida Keys, where in that last swoop

of paint drips—in a splash, Jackson Pollock couldn't

---

[16] If you are a believer in the linear nature of time, this poem is not for you. Congratulations, you figured that shit out in less than 21 full pages. Put the book down, walk away. For those of you in the future/past put the hieroglyphics down, put the Kindle down, put the Amazon sex robot down that's whispering tantalizing vowels at the part of your chin curving up from neck toward ear. If you are interested in breaking clocks though, check *Flatland: A Romance of Many Dimensions*, by Edwin Abbott Abbott, first published in 1884 by Seeley & Co. of London. Or check its Wikipedia page. Example from their "Critical Reception" section (as of 10/6/2016, or Hurricane Matthew's coming out party): "The book was discovered again after Albert Einstein's general theory of relativity was published, which introduced the concept of a fourth dimension. *Flatland* was mentioned in a letter entitled 'Euclid, Newton and Einstein' published in *Nature* on February 12, 1920. In this letter, Abbott is depicted, in a sense, as a prophet due to his intuition of the importance of *time* to explain certain phenomena."

possibly have planned—

they were safe and sound without even a Tropical Storm Warning.

Colored in with shades of red and orange depicting pending troubles, the remainder

of Florida was a paint-by-numbers map; Cat 1, Cat 2, Cat 3, Cat 4.; to the meme

of five cats blowing in, surrounded by the wind.

Brad's friend Kelly told him yesterday

that for the Six-Toed Cat restaurant next to Hemingway's House

if Brad made some art on tiles of cats, they'd sell them by the crate.

25

In context: Back in 1961, when Roy Lichtenstein was searching

for a parking spot, the MoMA featured the Aaron Copland's play-opera,

The Second Hurricane.

The closest the National Gallery came to avant-garde

American Art in special exhibitions was a retrospective of the Realist Thomas Eakins,

who was then dead nearly fifty years; an artist who'd studied art in Europe and propagated those teachings throughout his career.

Chinese art, European art, King Tut, Goya, Rembrandt, and *Eyewitness Etchings*

from the Civil War were the other offerings from the museum that year.[17]

26

His post-Berkshires river of an email missive continued:

Chapter Two. My 12-Step sense was dead on. That was a meeting at the church/cathedral

we drove by. Makes me proud I knew that somehow. I went back the next morning and

met some folks there at a 10 AM meeting who were very pleasant.

I imagined bumping into you two blocks from your house that next morning and you getting a restraining order on me. In the picture, I'm holding binoculars and an *Audubon Field Guide.* Audubon visited Key West. He also killed birds and inserted pipe cleaners under feathers to pose them for his rendering. There are ways I wish you were more like James Audubon and ways I hope you never are. I will let you discern.

---

[17] See *Big Red & Shiny*, by [REDACTED], "NGA: Roy Lichtenstein: A Retrospective" on December 16, 2012.

What about those hawks we saw outside The Clark?

MASS MoCA without you the next day: Anselm Kiefer. Oh my God. What

a triumph that is. I'd never seen it. Whoa. The universe pushed an older couple

timidly toward me in the exhibition hall. They asked if I knew what these

pieces 'were.' We had some fun. I acted as docent/counselor.

Melville's house is named Arrowhead. I had never heard that story you told me

about Greylock[18] and the whale's back before. How is it possible I'd never heard?

In random collage research, I once found a newspaper ad saying Melville had mail

waiting in the Sandwich Islands. It was just his name on a list of sailors.

---

[18]Mount Greylock is the highest natural peak in the Commonwealth of Massachusetts. "Melville is said to have taken part of his inspiration for *Moby-Dick* from the view of the mountain from his house Arrowhead in Pittsfield, since its snow-covered profile reminded him of a great white sperm whale's back breaking the ocean's surface." *("Herman Melville's Arrowhead," Berkshire Historical Society. Retrieved 2008-03-09).*

It was wonderful.

A guy at the 12 Step meeting mentioned in his share (unrelated to me) that he was

reading the book *Proper Bostonians.*[19] He explained there was a section about Isabela Stewart Gardner

having a string quartet (chamber music) practice in secrecy before

unveiling her house to onlookers. In *The Varieties of Spiritual Experience* by William James (a 12 Step foundation stone

for atheists and agnostics being able

to get comfortable with the recovery program), he apparently mentioned this music,

in the unveiling, as a spiritual experience.

I worked there. I taught there. I attended an 8-week training there. How did I

not know?

What about that Sargent? What about all that nudity? Suspin got all of those Rouen

Cathedrals on loan from 4 corners of the universe and showed them together once.

Oh Suspin.

---

[19] Cleveland Armory, Parnassus Imprints; Reprint edition (June 1984)

A woman rolls lettuce.

27

Some things everyone knows about time and time machines is the law of diminishing;

atmospheric perspective blurring excesses away. How could Brad have a computer

more powerful than the 1970s Strategic Air Command in the back pocket of his slim-fit

jeans (MADE IN VIETNAM) and not have

any extra time?

His trip Northeast became Jenga pieces slid together, falling down; his trip became

announcements of *Goodbye* and *Love you* in the guise of information ricocheted through train station egresses and bus

station bathroom stalls.

In an email to Francis Tarjee Suspin, he relayed the story of his

grandmom and her

love for the tallest mountain. "A quick

Mt. Greylock aside: My grandmother Helen grew up at the base. Her husband, my grandfather Red,

loved loved loved to travel. He owned a big Winnebago. And then another.

During the fuel rations of WW2, he traded for ration tickets to get to Cape Cod

and back in his roadster at the time.

"I come by road trips naturally.

"Well, he would get them to Florida, or California, or some

such, and my grandmother—

whose favorite Uncle Brad became my name inspiration—would start moaning

and crying; how much she missed Mt. Greylock. They would inevitably

have to turn around.

She took it almost viscerally years later when a fire scarred

the mountaintop."

28

Paintings Brad had once created with Lichtenstein in mind:

a series of cartoons filled in with x's and o's; snowflakes masquerading as Ben-Day dots, a road map between Rutgers and Leo Castelli's space

(possibly the most historic drive in American Art); music notes; OxyContin pills spilled in piles; noose holes; tie knots without the necks;

organic and inorganic cells. All of this started with an idea to widen Barnett Newman stripes and find the parallel universes there behind.

Instead, eventually, inevitably, Brad
inverted Lichtenstein.

Brad made painting dots from Chinese restaurant menus,
a schematic for an emotional '89 Dodge Caravan, his stepfather's model plane plans, a Victoria's Secret catalog,
scratched-off scratch tickets and
postcards too, Art History footnotes, and more.

For his solo exhibition
at the Federal Courthouse in Boston, a site he shared with Ellsworth Kelly,[20]
Brad filled brick walls with grand machines made up
of scattered dots. The spots themselves were the pictures,
the empty spaces
surrounding, a series of incomplete
and unrecorded memories.
Yes, Brad meant it. The greatest curating in the world of art
was placing Lichtenstein on an elevator landing pad.

---

[20] Brad knew it was time to quit his corporate gig when the people he worked with kept saying: "You're an artist. What do you think of those squares?" While speaking of Ellsworth Kelly. How could he explain forever to a beehive filled with shoe polish and Botox foreheads? He gave two weeks' notice and resigned.

29

The Gallery Director in Key West, at Brad's last[21]
juried exhibition,
described his collage work as "Lichtenstein on acid."

Brad wrote to Angela: Have you found the postcards
in your car yet?
While this is more efficient than mailing you the Sargent
as I had planned,
it lacks some of the emotional intent.

Brad wrote: I'm starting to have serious doubts
about sending this.

Brad wrote: So, I am not sure why it seemed like zero
big deal to come to see you.

I didn't give the Mass Pike trip a second thought. You are one of my favorite

people, and my trip was without premeditation or motive. Maybe it was missing the chance at your road trip offer last spring or missing

seeing you in Montana this time. Just seemed like what

---

[21] Last as most recent.

I should do.[22]

30

Context: Brad hadn't drank in 20 years when he saw the girl drowning

again; drowning this time, again,

anyway. Water, water, everywhere.

31

In Key West, he stopped at a traffic light. The red

made up of light dots;

green made up of light dots; the full moon

over Smathers Beach

impossible to render with a fingertip push

on iPhone screen.

In Key West, on Sundays, he pulled out her letter

to him, counted

white spots between the figures she'd scrawled

on the page.

The B, the a, the d; all of them drew dots.

---

[22] If you find an incidence of chaptered email missives, I will relinquish claim to the invention of the form.

When Brad was 30 and moved to the world

every Boston artist[23]

with limited imagination[24] used to wonder at—

Fort Point—he glued *Art in America* covers, ads, and exhibition

announcements in every section of his bathroom.

An automatic light with motion detector eyes,

crappy colored Japanese lanterns in different hues plugged in below,

cast pastel shades on art's most recent history. There, Andy Warhol's dance steps,[25] face looking down to make fun of (and bury) Jackson Pollock,[26]

stood sentry at the conventional light switch. For

---

[23] One night when Brad was less than a year sober and still not sleeping, stretched out on the couch of the apartment on Hemenway Street, he caught the part of *New York Stories* where Nick Nolte is an AbEx painter, plays basketball indoors, smears paint to hard rock music sounds. Brad thought, for the first time since he stopped drinking, he had a hope: I'd like to do that someday. 10 years later Brad looked up, living in a 1,300 square foot loft with slop sink and oil paint fumes wafting to tunes of *Yellowcard.* Brad also watched *Kicking and Screaming* (Stoltz not Ferrell) then, and fell in love with Noah Baumbach. Noah Baumach as a filmmaker and Jonathan Lethem as a writer are the two men Brad most associated with our generation's avant-garde.

[24] Brad couldn't have thought L.A. or New York City? Miami Beach?

[25] See Andy Warhol, *Dance Diagram, 5 (Fox Trot: "The Right Turn – Man")*, 1962.

[26] See Hans Namuth's photos of Jackson Pollock painting.

Warhol's dick, Brad let that

white nose spring from Andy's pants, hand on hip.

Turn on, turn on, *Turn on the night*

light baby.[27] There's so much more music to come. *Blue canary in the outlet by the light switch, who watches over you?*[28]

Brad wrote to no one in particular: American Artists post-WW2

are comic book characters in the cathedral of my mind.

What's more important as you get older; your clothes, or

soaped-up nudity? Or is it the toilet bowl

you aim for after painting into morning light?

32

Freckles; constellations, stars, and horoscopes. Coins

---

[27] None of the YouTube songs Brad looked up for this tune fit the melody in his mind. Fill in your own blanks. Be Cézanne but more decisive, even while uncertain. Stand farther back than your companions so the world is less curved and photographically distorted by the blue orb masquerading as your eye and play apple-edge-MadLibs.

[28] *They Might Be Giants,* "Birdhouse In Your Soul," from the album *Flood*, released in 1990. Do yourself a favor and watch the documentary *Gigantic: A Tale of Two Johns.* Then later, go to the free TMGB show at Border's Bookstore at Downtown Crossing in Boston. Flirt with a girl. Find out Kenneth Koch is dead. Brad did this too.

in the sky. Matisse under the Tahitian sea, finally realizing all fish were birds in bowls.

October 12 and Ihab Hassan[29] as part
of Brad's Daily Meditation:

> Unknowingly we plow the dust of stars, blown about us by the wind, and drink the universe in a glass of rain.[30]

(Water as droplet and stream).

33

Telephones have always been both single points and streams.

---

[29] Famous for the table of differences between Modern and Postmodern in *The Dismemberment of Orpheus: Toward a Postmodern Literature* (1971), what if Kent Johnson is wrong in his book *A Question Mark Above the Sun*, and Frank O'Hara really did write "A True Account of Talking to the Sun at Fire Island," and even wrote it before the estimate of 1955? Is there any doubt that *Target With Plaster Casts* by Jasper Johns is an image of his friend Frank O'Hara as Orpheus, dismembered by the local women for loving boys, and friends solely with the Sun in the end? What better symbol for a target than the Sun, and vice versa? What are you shooting for Cupid? Everything you cast your eyes on? The sky is a series of dots. All of us are exploding. (Hassan could have just written for his book, incidentally: "See Claude Monet").

[30] From *Wisdom to Know*, Hazelden, 2005.

Take a peek at mouthpiece and receiver on a corded-up phone someday. Push fingertip

into rotary dial holes, and search for braille dots on the ATM machine for miming

moves toward bankrupt. Telephone lines and telephone poles,

the prayers we used to speak out loud

for our current Google typing

and Okay Google explanations were once suspended across

the country in sprawling crucifix landscapes. She turned

on the porchlight.

34

We hadn't talked in a few days when you/she sent the email—

I mean a text message—to ask if I had to evacuate; if I

was ok. All of this came a week or so after I decided I wanted

to tell you everything. Again, not in a confession,

as the closest I've ever been to confession

is in the midst of the DTs while trying to get sober at St. Ignatius during a wedding. I slinked in

and stood in line. I drank communion wine.

What kind of religion makes it a sin to try and be one of them

unless you've already performed some other ceremony for salvation?

The Catholic Church as a dance instructor: Get up, Get down,

Get on your knees, now. My friend Pete Shoreword calls it the magic show.

No, I mean

I wanted to tell you everything because I wanted to share myself with you

so much I just couldn't; I couldn't stop talking.

35

She texted him the next afternoon: I should tell you

I have a phone phobia. At the very least, I don't like talking

on the phone.

36

I can see the blood. The tracks my fingertips make on smartphone glass when I get demanding for attention, for donuts, for the smear and smudge

of Google Map pointers despite this New York rain. I can see these meandering

fogs, a glance up Fifth Avenue when cathedrals caught in tipped horizon pray (money)

and pray (redemption)

in the change purse of the crosswalk.

In Manhattan, near Penn Station, a couple sets out their clothes, folded and dependable,

and argue about their home. Someone makes a promise and leads them far away.

We all come back as birds. See the dot get closer from horizon.

See the hawk.

See the dot get closer, seagull. See the seagull.

See the sky.

See the hole in the bottom of the shoe. See the blood; see the

shoelace eyes.

Sometimes the river of dots is tears or circumstance,

and sometimes the river of tar

is combined in destination minds, and sometimes

the dot getting closer

is a reincarnation of your father.

And sometimes the dot's an albatross.

What spots are your skies made up of today?

37

Brad's father always said:
"Wish in one hand and shit in the other
and see which fills up first."

38

Halfway through the middle of this trip
to the other end of America's Atlantic coast
Brad woke one morning in Plymouth, Massachusetts
and checked Facebook
through half a sleepy eye.[31] He shouldn't do this
before he prays. One thing
the world will do to you before it breaks you[32] is rile you up
about a bunch of shit
you have no business giving a second thought to.

By you, I mean Brad. By trip, I mean trip up to Boston
and Manhattan from Key West for two weeks; go on
retreat, see Mom, visit museums, and do speed-dating style
catch-ups with friends, family, former professors, and

---

[31] Two halves.

[32] See that Hemingway Meme for closure.

12 Step cronies.

By halfway through the middle, I mean halfway
through the middle
          of everything—the donut hole or the jelly,
depending on your preference about existence and God
          and where souls might reside in your current version of the multiverse.

Before Brad's grandmother died a few years back, he mused
          on the arc of her life from 1910 to 2013. Would anyone ever have a more startling dream for and of existence?

A birth at the foot of Mt. Greylock with no electricity to start,
          push on through World Wars 1 & 2,
          semi-indentured servitude,
German speech admonishments from family, and get
into spreading
          inventions like cars and indoor plumbing, electricity, and cable TV;
          the internet.

This was before Brad understood himself as dreamer, or got hit
          with arrows
          while standing near Angela, her world a porchlight
in Berkshires'

pitch. Angela's power, wrapped in perfect jeans and illusions of casual fragility, reminded him of the him he used to be; of letters

and telephones bolted to the wall; of books and answering machines

with miniature cassette tapes [BEEP];

of privacy, of intimacy, of plane rides unspooling sentiment

between stretched-out arms of parents. Angela reminded Brad

of leaving and arriving,

of mechanical unrest; of his trip, and of his life. Bus ride to train ride

to car ride

to home to play your life

back in reverse and press the button on a pre-voicemail machine [BEEP].

There are letters in your mailbox, waiting.

39

Brad already wished.

Brad already wished Angela and he

were Julia and George Clooney

instead of their actual famous namesakes

on every grocery store checkout

announcing a personal storm. His favorite line

in movies, was Clooney ordering a drink:[33]

"Whiskey / whiskey"

at the top of the casino floor.

"They are not our namesakes," Angela said.

"The word itself will tell it all:

She's a smaller version of me."

40

Brad once glued photocopies of postcards to a canvas, to a dozen canvases,

along with losing scratch tickets when first settling in, and sprawling out,

into his newest loft space in the soon-to-be gentrified

Fort Point. Brad

was halfway between landscapes. Today, less than a

---

[33] Brad always conflated this scene from the *Ocean's 11* remake with one from the Elmore Leonard book/movie with Clooney and J-Lo on the top floor of the Ren Center in Detroit (*Out of Sight*); the sky full of white circles like the bottoms of exclamation points in city skyline's night.

week after that open-eye Plymouth morning he kept coming
back to, he left Miami Beach and thought about construction.

He couldn't help but consider sand. But in the poem—
this odyssey—he hasn't left Plymouth yet.[34] When you
get a chance, redefine the word *begin.*

Brad woke that morning in Plymouth, the third town he had
ever lived in[35]

---

[34] I've been thinking of hand me downs lately after losing weight at the gym and watching what I eat. If you lose weight and don't buy new clothes, you look as though you are an adult wearing hand me downs. Today in a 12 Step meeting a man said he tried on a Louis Vuitton leather jacket at the store the other day. When Brad first got sober, he couldn't afford a winter coat. I wore a windbreaker and layered sweaters every day. Wherever he went he peeled layers off when he arrived. Angela does this with curating art shows.

[35] I was born in Scranton, Pennsylvania, made famous now by the American version of *The Office*. When I was growing up and adults heard "Scranton," they'd say, "The armpit of America," or "The asshole of America" depending on their comfort with children hearing curse words. I then moved to Castro Valley, California. We took a road trip when I was less than one year old. This was pre-car seat insanity. My folks put a crib in the backseat and I stood up and grinned the entire ride. Blame my wanderlust on nature—my genealogy of leavers—or nurture, with my early road trips and airplane rides. Either way I write this on a couch I only rented. At any point I could wake up and pack the car and show up on a doorstep. The last day Brad drank (I hope) he called his dad and made casual conversation about visiting him that summer. He thought it would help him stop doing drugs and drinking, but Brad didn't tell him that. Two days later in the psych ward Brad

and looked at Facebook too early. He was halfway through a halfway trip

of life, 42 years old and strands of white

in sideburns, sleeping in a guest room in his mother's house (in

his house).

Facebook mentioned Hurricane Matthew's indecision. It

wasn't the largest Atlantic hurricane to hit

in over ten years yet.

Matthew swirled up from South America

then, gaining rank from Tropical Storm status. It was a Tuesday. Before

he prayed, he thought:

a) If this hurricane hits Key West, maybe I don't have to leave. He thought, Surrender.

He thought, leave the shitty job cold calling Dog

Groomers, Plastic Surgeons, and disinterested Florists.[36] He thought, No one could ever blame you

---

spoke to him on the payphone. "I don't understand," his dad said. "We just talked the other day."

[36] As they always say, a red flag that you might not like your job is rooting for a hurricane. Can you keep up with the changes in terminology? Typhoons are hurricanes now? Blizzards are snow hurricanes? It's like my mother using the word "Oriental" and being bewildered when I admonish. She loves Hot & Sour soup. My father, who worked for the USDA, barely ever went out to eat. Knowledge is

who already signed up. He thought, the corporation would sever contracts, even with their missionary Tony Robbins, *Invasion of the Body Snatchers,* YouTube video style. "Culture is King," they'd say in unison.

"Get your mind right," they'd suggest, casually requesting he do something in a moment he'd been parsing out ineffectively for 42 years. He said,

"When I met Francis Tarjee Suspin, I was Vincent van Gogh recently sprung from San Remy. He helped to save my life."[37] Brad didn't say that then though. That quote was another memory, another post-elevator ride.

---

paralysis and hunger. Knowledge is seeing the sausage made without a metaphor in sight; just blood and intestines getting hosed off of your clothes at the end of the day.

[37] That's not true. I said that in an email introducing Angela to Francis. But for the purposes of this poem, and eternity, time is a Don Rickles roast. Time makes fun of you and then pretends to be your friend. Or, time is your friend and then pretends to make fun of you. Besides, I had to tell you early I'd graduated from a psych ward. How else could I establish poetic credibility? See the Webster's Dictionary guy. See Ezra Pound. Instead, see Hemingway pleading. See Dashiell Hammett. See Hemingway in Mayo Clinic on the other side of the handle-less doors. See Elmore Leonard's book *Pronto.* See William Carlos Williams visiting his friend in St. Elizabeth's. See me in a different St. Elizabeth's, panic attacks and psychotic episodes every day. The Head Shrink says, "Schizophrenic with a Psychotic Disorder." I'd expected, perhaps, a Cat Scan. Brad says, "I think I'm going to try 12 Step meetings." If I am counting, this is one of the miracles the universe performed. The universe is a miracle, my friend. Even when it's making fun of me.

b) I know she was worried about illegible handwriting, but what if Angela's letter is the victim of a deluge? Image: a handwritten envelope bobbing down Whitehead Street. There, a lighthouse. There, Hemingway's house, the makeshift mortar fence keeping out the tourists before something awful happens (fill in the blank mortar stones, Cézanne).

Tell me which is which. Flip to the back of the *People* magazine someone slipped you in a manila envelope and play the matching game.

Which is different? Which is the same?

c) He thought about the words "Come home, come home, come home."

41

Cue Track 9 from *A1A*, Jimmy Buffett's fifth studio album,

hear the song *Trying to Reason with Hurricane Season.*[38]

---

[38] My conch friends (A conch is a Key West local. Freshwater Conch is someone who has lived there 7 years or more. A Saltwater Conch was born and raised here) attribute the psychotic real estate market in Key West to a lack of recent hurricanes. "One good blower, and everything changes," my friend Motorcycle George told me recently. Although I had dinner with Heidi Blanksphere, a girl who loves chairs,

If you synch the tune up with this freeform poem before you,

the two will be choreography for *The Wizard of Oz.*

There's no place like home; there's no place like home.

True story: After Brad asked God for direction and went on retreat, a man who once trained to be a horse jockey (read, is kind of on

the short side), and later became a murderer (read, this is not a metaphor), and even later

became one of Brad's most trusted spiritual advisors (read, he

gut-shot

a man and then went to jail), said to Brad in his retreat house bedroom:

"Come home, come home, come home."

---

and she said a surfboard blasted through the wall of her grandmother's house like a missile during Hurricane Wilma. The flipping and gnawing fastball, propelled at 90 miles an hour, allowed enough destruction and pressurized air in the war zone to blow the roof of that heirloom clear off. Heidi's friends harass her about loving chairs. She collects them like animal lovers collect stray kittens if they stop off at the shelter for a second. Heidi's conch friends threaten traps of discarded furniture baited on her return commutes from work, placed on sidewalks and just off curbs. She counted recently and found 57 chairs in her little conch house. Understanding genealogy, the next time she went home, she began counting in her mother's house. All of us are reassembling some puzzle in our mind; connecting scattered dots.

42

He kept saying it. Mickey never told Brad to do anything

in his life

before that moment, that day. "Come home," he said.

43

On the Facebook interweb jumble the next Tuesday morning, a building hurricane

spun closer, swirling and raining away.

You already know what the eye of the storm looked like.

Brad began reading the words of repetition: Cone, Models, and Track. But the combination

of a Munchkin Land-like native and "There's No Place Like Home," eluded him

until now. *My life is a soundtrack lined up with a movie.*

This is art and poetry. Start the music, stare at your shoes.

There's no place like home.

Jimmy Buffett? Yes, Jimmy Buffett. Brad hated him

when Melody Stripenhold put in those mix tapes in High School. Gross.

But when he got sad at Syracuse, he'd listen to JB's CDs,

especially the box set,

and flip through photo albums,[39] drinking Milwaukee's Best bottles by lamplight and feeling tears stream down his face.

He'd walk up to pretty girls at 44's on Marshall Street after 3-8 PM Happy Hour (5 bucks all you can drink,

beer and vodka mixers) wound down, and say "

Will you ask the DJ to play *Boat Drinks*?"

His favorite conversation piece

was a meticulously broken in *The Game,* "G" hat, for

Cape Cod Community College. His most important relationship, by far,

was with alcohol.[40]

---

[39] I had photo albums too. When I went to college there was no internet, or Skype, or digital photography to speak of. My grandmother's life was a horse carriage ride. I live on a different planet, metaphorically future Mars-dwellers, than the one I was born to. Every 7 years the entire human body regenerates its cells. Who the hell am I? A man carrying a donkey with a horse problem.

[40] Mark and Ken used to buy a case of Milwaukee's Best every Friday, play Pitch, and listen to Bob Marley. Every Friday after they both finished 8 beers, one would flip a coin and call it heads or tails. The loser got an empty bottle broken over his head. One week, Mark hit sort of crooked and the bottle didn't break, only thudded against Ken's squash. His eyes turned black and blue like he'd broken his nose. One weekend, Ryan Grater came up to see Brad. Mark pulled him aside and said "Brad's drinking a lot. We're worried. You should talk to him." One of the guys who used his head as bottle buster thought Brad

It's sacrilege to like Jimmy Buffett and live in the Florida Keys, which I do now,

which Brad does now, despite those hurricane fantasies and hurricane surrenders. Despite future tripping to another Master's Degree

or Ph.D., or anywhere with Angela, Brad loved

Jimmy Buffett.

He hummed those songs as life's soundtrack without meaning to. They were in Brad's

blood and tendons, the tracks traveling through cells and DNA, across

back and legs and back again.

Listen:

This morning, I shot six holes in my freezer.

I think I got cabin fever.

Somebody sound the alarm.

Trace the song's origins back to Boston—track it back

with taxi cabs

and ice storms—and how could Brad not love? Snobbery in Key West

against Jimmy Buffett is no different than snobbery

---

was the one with a drinking problem. And he was right.

on Park Ave.

Brad's father, or my father, wearing cowboy boots, taught there was nothing wrong

with people thinking you were nowhere near as smart as you actually were.

He taught knowing how to fish and trap was as valuable as literary criticism.

And Brad decided against *Hurricane Season* despite the connection

and cued "Mother Mother Ocean, I have heard you call," from Track 7

of the same album. The song, *A Pirate Looks at 40.*

Sometimes when taking in the Southernmost Horizon Line from a beach chair

on Smathers or Higgs Beach in Key West I sing this too, or hum along with Brad,

before I know the music notes are spreading out inside of me.

Other Jimmy Buffett tunes I hum at random scored intervals of this donkey ride/

horse ride/train ride I call life include: "Island" and "Last Mango in Paris,"

"Growing Older But Not Up" and "Miss You So Badly

(Live)."[41] "Havana Daydreamin'"

and "Take Another Road" and "Incommunicado."

A painter looks at 42. Each of us discovers

the internal soundtracks

we've unwittingly soaked inside.

44

Brad just checked Facebook from a bus.

Right now, when Brad tried to text, his Samsung Galaxy

Note 4 froze and turned off. In the past months, he'd had a landline installed, purchased a new extra-capacity battery for his cell piece,

and had Wi-Fi issues galore (if you want your sponsor to cosign a resentment, mention Comcast frequently).

Brad had navigated various apartment moving issues, and now this. The world is not a kind communicator these days.

Angela's en-route letter

writing had a point after all. He was less than two hours from

the mailbox now. He told you time was a liar. Facebook watches Matthew.

---

[41] The Missoula reference on this version probably doesn't hurt.

They're predicting 40 inches of Haitian rain
and he kept worrying about making cold calls.

45

Brad's most recent Artist's Statement:

Alphabet Soup

My old friend Patrick, a former low-level gangster from South Boston, liked to say, "I used to think I was Al Capone. I found out I was just an alcoholic." They called him the Henny Youngman of Southie. When I went away to graduate school in Montana, I'd drop him a note from time to time. "I got your postcard from Colorado," he said when I came home over Christmas. There was Southie—then Cambridge, and a bunch of land—and then Colorado. I never corrected him.

Pat wouldn't wear his hair cut too short. "Over the years, I've been hit with so many bats and bottles and rocks; I even got shot in the back of the melon coming out of the projects one Sunday morning right in front of my mother. Got a crew cut once too. Looked like I had the whole alphabet drawn all over my head there are so many scars."

When I got out of lockup, they told me to get honest. So I was talking to my aftercare counselor at St. Elizabeth's as her eyes kept getting wider and wider. She finally sent me over to the

Head Shrink, and he basically just started saying crazy mixed-up letters for my diagnosis: A, B, C, D, PTSD. Then DTs, ADD, PAWS, Depression, Schizophrenia, Psychosis.

Patrick had an alphabet written on the outside of his head. I had one written on the inside of mine.

When I told him about the doctor, he said, "I used to think I was Al Capone—" You know the rest.

Before breathalyzers got big, Pat and I both passed a bunch of roadside field sobriety tests, even after drinking whole cases of beer. "Back then, before computers, you could just put a license plate on a new car. I kept finding cars that didn't belong to me," Pat said. The officer said to me, "Can you drive?" and I could barely walk. "Say the alphabet backward," he said. I knew I was home free. The key to saying the alphabet backward is the same as it is to successfully drinking tequila: Practice.

"I walked into recovery and thought, 'Don't you know who I think I am?' I was a rebel without a clue. Now I'm just another bozo on the bus; another noodle in the soup," Pat said.

I said, "Alphabet soup."

46

One Christmas after I left, Pat started shooting dope again, wrapping lines against his arm, wrapping noodles around his neck. They found him hanged in his living room three weeks after New Year's Day.

In my visual art, I try to find the lines sketching letters inside and outside my mind; the scars. And I try to untangle them before they kill me. My digital collages take familiar stories—Romances, Westerns, War—and combine them with my personal experience. Like when Pat got a haircut and everything was revealed, his past and maybe his present too, my collage works bridge my past with that of the audience.

I'm heavily influenced by my own physical landscapes, my destinations and arrivals, and lingering points, as well as by my emotional landscapes. After my parents got divorced, they split the country in half as the separation agreement. She took Boston and The Berkshires down to Florida and Siesta Key; he took California's Bay Area up to Montana. The Mississippi River served as the symbol of their broken heart. The Mississippi River is the symbol of my broken heart.

When Dwight Eisenhower returned from World War II, he commissioned Jackson Pollock to splatter black tar paint all over the country, a giant stomping all over the Great Plains. In my work, there are emotional and physical maps, the lines of highways, and flight paths. There are the maps of Historical Fiction and fantasy; Arshile Gorky refused to look at the Grand Canyon one time when he drove cross country, incensed God would challenge him in drawing a perfect line.

47

All of my work is informed by Art History. Monet's later landscapes—the grand lily decorations where he simultaneously painted the surface of the water, the reflection of the sky, and the roots and murk below the surface, depict three different spaces in the same single picture plane—informs any multiverse our scattered cells inhabit. This shift from flat to deep, reflected to penetrating, internal to external, shows up again and again in my works. Cultural identity, personal identity, sexuality, violence, and emotion are embedded. My hope is viewers and readers find a different part of themselves on each visit, as with returning to a place you love or hate; or in finding a new landscape for the first time that feels like home.

When I got a job at the Isabella Stewart Gardner Museum in Boston, the site of the infamous Rembrandt robbery, Pat took me aside one day. He said, "If you ever want to know the guys who did it, let me know."

I never asked. Those blank spaces are still hanging all around my walls.

48

What separates the word from the world is a single letter

L. Love the word, and you create the world. Everything we've ever thought of came into existence too. *Back to the Future*

ideas and Brad watching

MacGyver get remade. The world is a remake of a remake. God

said be like me: *Create.* We recreate instead. The world
is a collage. The world

is a skipping record. In the beginning, was the word. In
the beginning,

was an equation. Just add up the love.

Airplanes, cars, trains, and buses. I have trouble believing

Frank O'Hara

got summoned over bus station intercoms years beyond
his death.

All of us know the lies all painters tell when met with beautiful

departures. If any ghosts are boarding,
it's definitely on a train.

Thirty minutes in a museum. I haven't made New York

yet. In reality, I just left Philadelphia. In this book, I'm

in Key West. When two things come together, ice and liquid,
drink and glass, fire and eyes,

your seat near chamber music, these intersections slow,
go slower, touch. Everything good begins with a tuning fork-
sounding clink,

I'm sure the world misspelled.

49

Overheard at a 12-Step meeting: "Out of all the slogans

here on those blue and yellow banners—*First Things First, Think Think Think, One Day at a Time,*

Easy Does It—my favorite thing to read at meetings

has always been the EXIT sign."

50

Brad traveled with a finger puppet of Ernest Hemingway,

called him Little Hem. He got tired of taking selfies on cross-country trips and got tired

of ruining relationships with women on cross-country trips, so he slipped Little Hem

in his pocket a few years after cousin Constance gifted him for Xmas and they'd been all over social media ever since.

After Brad recently listened to an audio version of Steinbeck's

Travels with Charley, stunned at the beauty of the book, he had to buy a paper copy to read

and feel as well. He thought, "I got beat to the punch." Gary Sinise narrated.[42]

---

[42]One of my current can't-miss movies is *Forrest Gump.* If that sucker is on TV and I catch it, I have to watch the whole way through. I always tear up when Lt. Dan shows up at the wedding and Gump says "You got new legs." Also, I named a guy in an unpublished novel of mine

51

Julian Schnabel had Lichtenstein tantrums,

took plates shaped like Lichtenstein's early circle dots

and shattered them in paint.

Schnabel once said about Frank Gehry's critics,

If you can't compete with the architecture

of a museum, you might want to find

another line of work.[43]

Lichtenstein and the elevator girl were working.

Lt. Dave, just because. Also-also, when Lt. Dan screams at God, bobbing in the sea, it's the best impersonation of my early relationship with a Higher Power that I have ever seen. Yes, I have legs. No, I never bobbed in the ocean. But God. Oh, God. [I have self-diagnosed with ADD and more importantly, Emotional ADD (from the poem "Another Train" I wrote in reference to Kenneth Koch's death, trains, long distance love, and the T Conductor from Southie who once hit a guy who jumped in front of the Red Line approaching Broadway. Chewed the guy's flesh up and knocked his sneakers off)]. My friend Frank Casperato in Missoula, Montana, who we called Diamond Tooth, and who hid tequila in his garden hose for sipping on hot summer days, used to say 'I went back to school and got a bunch of degrees, so now I have all these letter after my name, BA, MA, PhD. You know what else has a lot of degrees? A thermometer. You know where you put a thermometer? Up your ass. In my case, PhD stands for Piled High and Deep because I'm full of bullshit.'

[43] This is a misquote. See Sony Pictures Home Entertainment's *Sketches of Frank Gehry* (2006) for clarity.

52

In the photo, Brad's reflection on the black mass of

Lichtenstein's *Drowning,*

he'd posted to Facebook, Brad's friend April

asked "Who's the mystery girl?" Even though she obviously meant the reflected

woman in the glass of the frame, Brad looked up

from his smartphone screen and wondered how she knew.

He was still sitting on a bench outside a Modern Museum Café

and considering the nature of the rain. Time is an elevator ride

to the beach.

53

Brad's father always said:

"If you're looking for sympathy, it's right there

in the Dictionary somewhere

between shit and syphilis."

54

According to Google, "Cathedral" as a word has dropped steadily off in mentions and usage since 1900. They have a line graph beginning in 1800 wobbling around, presumably

measuring print media occurrences.[44]

Then the Industrial Revolution happens. Monet is born.

Monet builds a lily pond. His landscapers do, at least. He stares.

He stares. He stares. You should see the spike in 1900

when you enter the words: lily definition.

55

Brad thought, I left postcards in your car that I bought

in the gift shop of the Clark Art Institute while you searched for possible jewelry for superstar artist Tess Toro. When I arrived

in Key West, they were there too, along with your handwritten note and a copy of *Art Whirl*, in my post office box

packed up and bent with junk mail, magazines I never

---

[44] Okay Google: Cathedral, Cathedral, Cathedral. Will one rise up from ground; dissolve down from sky? The world is a construct by Okay Google and Siri gods. The movie *Beetlejuice* (1988, The Geffen Film Company) will clear up any questions about saying things in threes you may have. According to Wikipedia there is an unproduced sequel titled *Beetlejuice Goes Hawaiian.* Okay Google: "Beetlejuice Goes Hawaiian, Beetlejuice Goes Hawaiian, Beetlejuice Goes Hawaiian."

subscribed to,[45] and trinkets

from the Chamber of Commerce, waiting.

Postcard 1 is *Rockets and Blue Lights (Close at Hand) to Warn Steamboats of Shoal Water* (detail), from 1840 by Turner. Brad didn't see this picture at The Clark, usually a no-no when

investing in gift shop

mementos used as mailers, bookmarks, refrigerator magnets, or surprises

down the line when he revisited piles of memories in drawers or shoeboxes.[46]

His friend Kelly, who he saw tonight at his first meeting back

in Key West, just finalized his move out of a house he'd

shared with his partner of 30 years. "More traumatic

---

[45] Somebody apparently subscribed me to *Sports Illustrated* and *Vanity Fair.* I would guess jilted lovers, but no jilted lovers have my PO Box number. Jilted is an underused word.

[46] My best example of this is a golden hued San Francisco postcard I'd written to myself on what I'm guessing was my first trip out west to spend the summer with my father when I was 6 years old. On the backside, without a stamp, I'd addressed this carefully in a childish version of the awful handwriting I've progressed further toward illegibility since elementary school with each passing notebook, word, and year. The message says, "By the time you get this you'll be home," and I signed my name. Every time I find the picture in a stash of papers or a moving box, I flip it over once again and it breaks my fucking heart.

than a death in the family," Brad said.[47]

The reason for Turner is the strapping to a ship's mast; is the fight with Claude Monet; is landscape painting as a cathedral. Is riding

a Rumi Donkey and knowing everything in the tempest

may never—or may always—be ok.

56

Brad left his last apartment in a rush. The Physical Therapist

who he rented from, who had rubbed his feet

and told him about her tenure as a pageant winner

in her adolescence, when she said, "Did I ever tell you I was Little Miss Tennessee?"

She needed to come back early from Chattanooga,

and the prospect of sharing an apartment with her deaf

---

[47] If you check to see if your coffee maker's unplugged three times before you leave the house, do you have OCD or a bad memory? I ask because I am not sure if this quote on emotional distress is true. It sounds right though. When I was in Saint Elizabeth's, fresh out of the looney bin, they had me take a test on traumatic events in the past year with ratings as to their impact. Death of a Loved One, Death of a Pet, Moved, Started New Job/School. I broke the test. Best score I ever got. If that test had been the GRE's I'd have a PhD from Yale or Cal Berkeley right now. But part of what makes moving so hard is those shoeboxes. I go through each and every one to see if it's unplugged.

and diapered dog, not to mention the waning
spotlight of an unintentional former JonBenet Ramsey
impersonator who he'd shelled out countless copays to
return some flex to his basketball
mangled ankles for didn't entirely appeal,
and had Brad scanning classifieds; scanning classifieds and
squirming, complaining, calling everyone he knew in
Key West, stressing, and staring
down at the pit in his chest; staring down at the end of art,
Jackson Pollock's grave.

57

How can you continue to worry if every single time the world
delivers you away? Like going to a restaurant in a huff,
begging, yelling at the chef to make sure they've not run out of
food. Every single day you go. Every single day they
have plenty of food.[48]

Once in a while, they don't have exactly what you choose
to order. You eat,
and discover the cuisine is delicious; even better
than the dish you'd had in mind. Every time. Every time.

---

[48] If Brad knew how to reconcile this with actual famine and war and pestilence he'd be a genius, not a painter.

Every single

fucking time. You walk into the restaurant, glare at the chef, and growl.

God, forgive my worry.[49]

58

Brad's father always said:

"Oh yeah? And people in hell want ice water."

59

Right before Brad signed a lease at Ocean Walk,

he strolled out,

and called another Property Manager who hadn't returned his voicemail.

CLICK.

She could meet in 15 minutes. CLICK. He could move in

this weekend. CLICK. The house

was pink. CLICK. CLICK. CLICK.[50]

---

[49] "Worry is like sitting in a rocking chair. It's a lot of work, but you don't get anywhere."

[50] God is a clock. God is a combination lock. God is my Cupid, my

He didn't notice until a few days

after he moved into his house, halfway

between Hemingway's house and the Southernmost Point in the Continental

USA, the lawn decorations his landlady had left in the rocky garden.

There on three tablets:

The footprints prayer

on his front lawn.[51]

60

[What if your cupid wielded harpoon spears?]

The first part of Brad's daily Rumi poem titled *A Trace,* from the Coleman Barks

---

manager, my investment banker, my compass, my chef.

[51] For those unfamiliar, the Footprints Prayer is a staple of 12-Step communities. The three plaques on Brad's lawn contain the last part of that prayer: "Lord, you said that once I decided to follow you, You would walk with me all the way; But I have noticed that during the most troublesome times in my life, There is only one set of footprints. I don't understand why in times when I needed you the most, you should leave me. The Lord replied, 'My precious, precious child. I love you, and I would never, never leave you during your times of trial and suffering. When you saw only one set of footprints, It was then that I carried you.'"

translation *A Year With Rumi,*[52] dated September 30.

This was his year two

with this Rumi[53] book, integral to his morning meditations. He read in Plymouth,

cross-legged on the floor:

You that give new life to this planet,
you that transcend logic, come.
I am only an arrow. Fill your bow with me
and let fly. Because of this love for you,
my bowl has fallen from the roof.[54]
Put down a ladder and collect the pieces.

[What if your cupid posed as boatheader in a whaleboat
rolling up and down in a life full of black tar rivers
collapsing like the sea?]

---

[52] HarperOne. New York, 2006.

[53] Angela always mentioned Rumi when she wrote about Persian Art it seems. Spiritual, simple, complex, direct and tight, he may have been the first true poet, an honor Brad once reserved for Donne.

[54] I always think of that Arshile Gorky story about "Goats on the roof." Where is this from? What is the context? What does it mean? Poor guy hanged himself. Alcoholism and paint fumes. At Bill de Kooning's first big show, Gorky showed up, and complimented him on the frames. See Eidsvig's novel, "Art Official" and the story of Adolphe Gurkus and Billy Keening for more on the hijinks of this duo.

[Drive south between Routes 7 and 9, somewhere down near
Pittsfield, getting lost. And spy Melville's home there,
where he stared out at Mount Greylock, the
monster covered
with snow in winter, emerging from the wood.
My grandfather's whale; my grandmother's whale.
I'm sinking.]

61

(The Wednesday 10/5 before Hurricane Matthew)

[Overneat hours] [They watt until the last minute]
[We are starting to feel
a few of the bands]
[I have been listening as closely as we can]

Watch TV on an elliptical[55] in the gym to catch Closed
Captioning mistakes, and no one knows you're a
painter in a hurricane. They believe
your grieving eyes are terrified. They stop, and watch
your expressive
lines shooting arrows at the mounted screens. [There's

---

[55] See the definition of ellipses. See three dots. See pedaling toward infinity.

telling everyone

to get to the second floor] [The stranded flight
crews. There's a flood at the door knocker] [There
are goats on the roof.] When I got to The Berkshires, I didn't know what door
to knock on. [What's your plan for your family tonight?]

[(No response)]

[There's a Dunkin' Donuts still open for business in Nassau.]

You drive by the sign, press down on the anti-lock brakes
in time,
your phone is on the fritz, and the signal is in decline.

[Arrowhead] Arrowhead, you read the sign. Your phone
won't ring.
[I'd rather sink]

62

Personal injury lawyers and Rooms 2 Go ads
without phonetic typos commercialize
the size of storms.
No Closed Captioning, and then [Captain we know her

under a Tropical Storm] Brad saw Pollock jabbing downward strokes with hands—javelin spears and harpoon blasts—drawing

on slips of paper. Jackson Pollock weeping at *Guernica* every day.

James Rosenquist at MASS MoCA,[56]

a hurricane swirl in ink. Make a loop. Get hanged.
Water water everywhere, and Angela would rather sink.

63

Look now at the porchlight.

INSERT rain on the surface

INSERT a field of destinations and arrivals

as landing points for looks and eyes and sighs

and explanations. In museums, Brad took

photos of the Exit Signs. He captured graphic designs

of historical women and men stuck to bathroom doors.

Brad Instagrammed maps with red dots marking 'You Are

---

[56] See *The Swimmer in the Econo-Mist*, from one of the first exhibitions at the MASS MoCA, and one of the first exhibitions Brad took in from the site of the former Sprague Electric where his grandmother worked after World War 2. She threw harpoons at Red, said they preferred her in the factory. Pollock really did cry. The Rosenquist is amazing, truly; swirls of ink in billboard artscape; Picasso's famous horse crane-necked and screaming at the outrage of shattering sky.

Here.' Every artwork with colored

circles becomes a Baldessari. The tourists started wondering

if Brad knew something that they didn't.

Ken Willis showed up on retreat late, looking like that kid,

Rail[57] from Southie.

(If you've ever seen a junkie stab his arm

with the teeth

of needles or dopeheads crossing Mass Ave to score Methadone in the morning,

you'll understand the resurgence of vampire and zombie movies). If you ever

go to Catholic Mass,

you'll know red and white,[58] blood and flesh, pills and

resurrection.

Before every meeting at St. Bridgid's,[59]

---

[57] I don't remember Rail's real name, but am pretty sure he's still alive, He was so strung out and skinny everybody called him Rail. Only problem, he did a little time. He did a little too little time. He got out and everybody knew for certain the kid was a rat. You would rather be a Quaker shunned come barn raising time than Rail in Southie then.

[58] One of the recurring hallucinations Brad had during the worst of my bouts with the DT's: red and white. Marlboro packs. Communion wine and wafers. Brake lights. Paper.

[59] No one is 100% sure how they lost the hall at St Bridgid's back then. Some say the janitor almost got poked by hypodermic while taking out the trash. Some say Missy Indigo—who ran a gambling ring with new

back when Brad's father

had Stage 4 Cancer,[60] Brad went over to the chapel, pulled out the kneeler,

clasped hands and prayed. A few months later,

he realized when he prayed

for his dad—and prayed for him,

and prayed for him,

and prayed—

Brad had prayed for him to die.[61]

64

---

young dudes in the program—told the priest to fuck off when he asked her to not smoke in the courtyard at the break. Some say Noodles Campbell left the infamous needle in the trash. Either way, all the meetings eventually got displaced so it probably wasn't one thing. NOTE: At this point in this poem about New York I know it's actually about South Boston, Just like I knew before I started, all of it was meant for you.

[60]My father looked like the Marlboro Man.

[61] My friend Peter Shorewood in Southie, a guy who survived Korea and then a 30-plus year career with DSS (he was the guy who goes in the house and sees the filth and walks out with the kids) is a recovering Catholic and calls mass "The Magic Show." He's a poet and watercolorist. He's one of the kindest and gentlest and toughest men I know. He loves my poem "Counting," and encouraged me to date this film producer when the girl moved back to town. "You've got the chops," he said, "for now." She loved a second-generation mob guy. Someone Craig Finch used to pay a cut to when he ran a corner up City Point.

During a Lichtenstein phase, or one of his empty spots
between them,
Brad used hole punches to create cheese grater Ben Day
patterns on bright white pages. Instead of keeping the marked-up sheets, the stenciled
remains, Brad filled Number 10 envelopes with white dots and wrote explanations
on their outsides: *Variations on a Theme*
By Lichtenstein;
Thursday Night; Oh, Brad; Relentless Valentine.

In Melville's book [spoiler alert], written with sunshine
striking mountain sides in the distances,
like harpoon barbs thrown
down through blubbered hides or Cupid shafts persistent in their missives,
Ishmael is the only one who survives.
Call me Ishmael,
Brad realized. Call me
Ishmael.

65

Toss rocks at the water until ripples reappear. Concentric rings
wade off, the stones collapsing surfaces. We head

for the bottom and don't see the wreckage left. Gulp breaths
        and sink, and spin, fight oxygen trajectories and hold.
And above you,
        when the weather breaks, is an image of a thousand
thousand dots becoming something else. Clink, clink, clink on
        the tin roof of this Key West house, the sounds begin
to multiply. You be the striking. I'll be the reflection coming
toward you,
        both of us moving away.

The way it works, you end up making other things
stand in place
        for the stuff you miss the most. Like when Brad
sent people to look at *Drowning Girl* to count her face
        in raindrops, or when he would go
to Missoula, Montana, or Flathead Lake and talk to his father.

These were surrogates for other spots, other spaces to
        fill up, and other punched-out
empties stacked up in compost heaps, recycling.

66

Brad went to Boston off and on during the trip up north. He
        met Francis Suspin in a Starbucks on Atlantic Ave.
Prior, he had walked down past Faneuil Hall, marveled

at Ai WeiWei's *Zodiac Heads* on the Rose Kennedy Greenway. In the background of every panoramic shot,

the Customs Tower looms; the Customs Tower, the old Federal Building, whatever you want to call it. Either way, they

telephoned someone in that office in the early '70s, and asked them to pick up

this Montana shit-kicker from the airport.

Sure enough, Dexter Eustis, originally from the northern part of Maine, spied

a guy in a Stetson hat and big silver belt buckle—rattlesnake boots and a plug of Skoal in-between his lower lips

and cheek—come strolling through Arrivals.

Brad's father's first office in

the Northeast was in Boston, Massachusetts, somewhere behind that round-faced clock machinery, a backdrop

for Ai WeiWei.[62]

---

[62] I asked you, and anyone reading this, earlier what were your cathedrals. A few years back Brad went to the Roy Lichtenstein Retrospective at the National Gallery in Washington D.C. He expected it to change his life but it didn't. He walked across to the Hirshorn after and saw an exhibition of Ai WeiWei, which he expected to be silly due to all the publicity around his political arrest. That man built cathedrals.

67

Brad's father worked at that building when his parents met.
They were on a double date with another couple, each of them
dating central casting's extras for the purposes
of this story.
A group of guys harassed her, extra pretty in any light.
They said she looked like *Misty*—or the girl
from the movie
Play Misty for Me; Jessica Walter and his mom,
both of them in their youth. His mother, dark-haired and petite.
Years later Brad's stepfather[63] called her
The Queen of the Berkshires.

Brad's father, a walking-talking mashup
between a Marlboro Man
billboard, Robert Redford, and JFK
went up to these dudes
and offered to knock the living shit out of them
if they didn't shut the fuck up.

---

[63] Brad's stepfather is buried beneath the stone in Cheshire on the left side of the bed. His mother's spot is saved, with a blank space left where God can provide a write-in candidate for year.

Later, whenever that cowboy and that movie queen

impersonator strolled into a bar on Cape Cod—these places filled with live music,

cigarette machines in hallways, and brandy snifters stuffed with ones on piano tops—the piano man meandered

into "Misty," and then "The Green Green Grass of Home" for Brad's country bumpkin dad.

68

Brad's father's cancer arrived in spots before filling in

strong and solid

and undeniable from any distance back.

When Brad's former counselor described a lack of perspective

she said *You're standing too close to the picture.*

Sometimes the dot you see approaching is a seagull.

And sometimes, it's an albatross.

69

When Brad got to MoMA, he decided to find paintings in the hallways. Not just restroom signs, but the work people walk by between careful exhibitions; Elevator Paintings, Escalator Paintings, Café Paintings.

Across the way from Lichtenstein gasping "Brad," the elevator doors slid open. Behind every work of art is another hidden world.

A girl commanded her friends to stare at Barnett Newman's *Vir Heroicus ublimis,* from 1950-1. "It shakes," she said. "It shakes." God would never shake. It's you who feels the trembling.[64]

If we have a girl, let's name her Dorothy.

70

My Father & Charlie Russell / My Mother Collected O'Keeffe:

Brad's biography of art before he arrives at MoMA.

---

[64] What is the name of the optical illusion phenomenon where your eyes move in the face of stillness? The one that explains the sight of UFOs? People in the darkest skies see a single point of light, their eyes wobble and see floating, flying, spaceships. People see fireworks. People all around you fall in love. Tonight a man at the Clark Institute sees you gasping at the cello strings (lines, railroads, highways) played with arrowheads combusting. Other catalysts for UFO sightings: weird clouds, lightning, and missile tests. "Hundreds of people in Manhattan's Chelsea neighborhood saw a cluster of silvery, shiny lights glittering from above. Naturally, initial descriptions of the supposed UFO varied wildly: Some folks reported seeing one large, slow-moving object full of lights, while others say they saw nearly a half-dozen entities. The strange, shimmering lights turned out to be caused by 12 helium balloons that escaped from an engagement party held for a teacher at the Milestone School in Mount Vernon, Westchester County, about 15 miles away" (*Live Science,* by Bjorn Carey and Remy Melina, November 10, 2010, 12:25pm ET).

My father collected clown figurines and Charlie Russell

reproductions. Just last month, Jack mentioned *It Ain't Meat Until It's In The Pan*

and Brad knew his father's ghost needed to speak.

He once called every Sunday.

The two tied themselves together in phone lines. So when Brad dialed

Angela last week, this standing on the edge of creek meant he needed to grab

and touch her. *Reach out. Reach out and touch someone.*

He'd studied this ad campaign at Syracuse his first semester, the

importance of casting actors in vignettes. Every morsel of a picture becomes a story.

The postcards he left in her car, he explained,

"You could collage."

[Once, I held an end of this wire in a telephone jack

inside my bedroom wall, trying to invent a way

to escape. When the phone rang, vibrations chewed and

chomped through muscles—tendons—in my arm]

71

Behind the wall, Jasper Johns has three paintings
on the 5th Floor.
Brad fantasized about art with endless footnotes.

A map- sized scale of one-to-one. Insert here, Alfred Barr and
Jasper Johns,
the MoMA collecting three of your paintings at age 27.

Back to Brad's father: Despite his lack of artistic sophistication,
he had an enormous Wyeth reproduction framed in his living room for his entire life. *Christina's World;* how that man felt before leaving, Montana
and everything after. Now tell me what he didn't know about art.

The 5th Floor Wyeth hangs beside a Hopper with house sides
the same pigment as the sky, a red-orange rusted railroad track divides this life from the other. Stand on top, and
the opposite occurs. Every person you've ever met is lying down, beside, or on, standing still or running, on a world
incised by railroad
ties. Find an advancement in America that won't increase our
woes, one unmarked by propaganda.

I fear democracy's days were numbered as soon as information
became so rapid in streaming deluge, the facts
sunk and disappeared.

72

Johns, these three paintings, these hallway decorations,
covered in cross-
hatched stripes. A skull, a scrotum. But the quality
of line reminds of a man on hands and knees pleading for a spring.

Five stripes
like fingertips smashing at the wall, searching for a mouth or ass,
an opening, just check the dotted line and sign.

You sent a note card, and I can hardly move to ask
could it be because you miss me?

73

On the train, the windows have the benefit of leftover raindrops
stuck to the polarized glass. Every hue of blue in the

reclining[65] sky

saturates against the ground; extends, unfolded, into scenarios

of clouds and green grass. Florida's peninsular accusatory finger[66]

points[67] down in shame, limp, and regretless.

---

[65] I of course refer to reclining in those tri-folding beach chairs only professional tanners and beach bums could ever hope to get slightly right. The awkward unfolding, the readjustment. Today the Florida sky clicks back aways and readjusts, burns its back thighs on heat, and then the rain falls. This rain could be rice on counter tops spilling out in coarse abundance. When I shave in train mirror, I hear the grains of hourglass blasts against each other. All of us are raised on parlor games with lessons that time reclaims all bones, swallows them in increasing deserts.

[66] Brad sent Chuckie Klimt and some others a text message with a photo of a poster from the Mustard Seed club in Manhattan I took on Friday. The poster reads, "The Kingdom of Heaven is like a grain of mustard seed which a man took + sowed in his field. it is the smallest of all seeds, but when it has grown it is the greatest of plants + becomes a tree, so that birds of the air come + make nests in its branches." Brad wrote to him (and the other friends he sent this to), "I am reflecting on you and the birds collected in your tree." Brad also sent Chuckie a photo of a finger pointing down a modest staircase. "The Mustard Seed" it reads on a yellow field. 2 minutes ago Chuckie sent Brad a Facebook message: "You posted this this week. In church this morning the gospel was on the mustard seed. Is HP trying to tell me something?" Brad met Chuckie Klimt at Mass General Hospital twenty years ago. He helped save Brad's life. He also has artworks of Brad's, collages of Superman comic backgrounds, hanging in his home. He was at Jack's first meeting too. The world is a cathedral. I'm still on the train writing. Almost to Palm Beach.

[67] The MoMA had a t-shirt Brad carried around but didn't buy. Lichtenstein's finger pointing. A finger without an Uncle Sam behind. Overheard in a meeting: if I point the finger I need to take a look at myself, I have three pointing back at me. Overheard in a meeting: If I

Since abandoning that in-progress stanza for footnote meandering, you

texted me back four times. I sent another shot of train-side glass and HD

smartphone camera filters. The same text four times. The train disagrees

with SMS. You're in a supermarket in The Berkshires.

Angela: I hope not everything I type

is x4. I'm in the grocery

store

That's weirdly lovely with

the window rain

Brad: That was taken that

moment for your window

longing sample. And no

---

point the finger, I have four pointing back at me. (Any topic can be an argument in meetings. There is no rhyme or reason as far as Brad could tell on who might count the thumb). Today Brad posted a photo of Little Hem upside-down in front of a window on the train. Brad wrote "Caption This," instead of Brad's instinctual "Caramba!" Someone wrote "I need the finger please." Brad's felt racist. His felt obscene. Facebook is for lovers. Was I happier before Facebook became extension cords on linoleum floors?

dice on the four times. The Florida
sky has been doing a MT
impersonation today. Lots
of sprawling and reclining.

74

This morning Brad woke up on the train back to Miami and imagined painting

images of elevators around the world. Paste-ups of elevators. The elevator across

from Lichtenstein—the Jasper Johns hands pleading for an escape

around the corner—had Brad thinking all of art history
was a series of elevators.

He also made a note to remember Perry Street and the Asian

girl posing in front

of a chain-link sign pleading with tourists to be gentle on the steps. 12 Steps

from Perry Street and the workshop, the sign, "There's no wrong way to get sober,"

and Brad looked the spot up on his smartphone. Who could it be? Some

Victorian novelist? No, it was the house they used for Carrie Bradshaw's

on *Sex in the City*. Anything can be your mecca.

Anything that can be

your cathedral, can be.

75

On retreat, the nun asked us to decorate an elevator. I put in

lilies, red walls; velvet couches. We rode this elevator in our minds down to the beach, met

and spoke with our higher power sitting on a piece of driftwood. I've been

doing a variation every day since. An elevator[68] can be a cathedral. See

the footprints on the beach.

76

At the Basquiat: A top of escalator crowd moved people

Mounds around the viewfinder composition,

the demands of Instagram

and Facebook status thoughts. Brad took a photo of the map

that said YOU ARE HERE, afraid anyone knew he was not. He could have told Angela in North Adams about

---

[68] According to a *New Yorker* article in April 21, 2008 Issue *Up and Then Down: The lives of elevators,* by Nick Paumgarten, elevators are basically the safest mode of travel in the world. This is a poor summary.

Velazquez combinations: Get a sketchbook,
a glass, ice shavings, and Degas.
Get Manet and dark lines
and a misremembered painting by that Spanish master. If you
gulp fast enough, Impressionist splotches could cover
your clothes and flesh and recast the whites of eyes.

You could become a leopard's skin.

When you turned the light on outside your house, did it say
"I'm safe,"
or "Come In?"

Painters know the foundation stone
of lyrics is covered
with emoji grins. There's a sign on the information booth
downstairs at MoMA.
It reads: YOU BELONG HERE. The hurricane, the theme
songs, the long length
of road depositing in Adams. You know the universe, its vote.

Democracy is crazy when you realize I couldn't find your book
about art at the Barnes and Nobles on 5th Ave.

If I explain too much, I miss you.

77

Movies with elevators as cathedrals:

Die Hard, The Departed, Ocean's 11.

"The all-glass Wonkevator in *Willy Wonka.* It was awesome

and scary at the same time. Plus, Charlie realized all his dreams were coming true."

Someone sends a YouTube clip of the elevator scene from *The Matrix.* "In *Elf,* he gets excited watching the buttons light up, and I think first

he does a Christmas Tree shape; then he just presses all the buttons.

I like to do that too, but only if it's just my friends in the elevator."

The Secret of My Success: Michael J. Fox.

Flight with Denzel. He has this nosebleed in an elevator, drops of blood—you know—when he's on his way down. Real subtle.

[OPENING DOORS] "The elevator was also a crucial part of the first few *Mad Men* seasons. Like when Pete

Campbell realized

the buying power of black consumers, or when Don got his revenge on Sterling."

"There's that one scene at the end

when the elevator doors are open and the empty beckoning abyss

of a shaft is there

waiting. *Inception,*

You've Got Mail,

Suddenly Last Summer, The Shining,

Drive.

"There's an interesting moment in *Bruce Almighty*

where Morgan Freeman tells him—this impersonator God—the elevator's broken. He ends up having to take the steps."[69] Tangentially, the most famous telephone booth

in the world is Superman's. All phone booths are Superman's cathedrals.

But the most important phone booth in the world, in

---

[69] All culled from friend's responses when Brad wrote: "Facebook universe: Favorite movies (or un-favorite movies) where elevators play a pivotal role? What are they (and *why* are they is extra credit). Feel free to PM me if you're more comfortable that way. I'm working on a Walt Whitman rip-off collage and your responses could help keep the poetic tradition alive while perhaps offering me 10 or 20 dollars in royalties over the course of my life."

the entire universe,

is the time machine in *Bill & Ted's.* All cathedrals are part-time time machines.

78

Water molecules; champagne bubbles, the bottom of a broiling pan. Brad inverted

dots. He inserted pictures in the empty. Brad's father always said:

"Wish in one hand

and shit in the other, and see which fills up first."

79

Brad received a text message from Angela. He called;

pictured her

on Robert Frost roads under Alex Katz skies, glintless eyes searching

yellow blinking lines.

[When the ship moved out from harbor,

locals reported omens in their sphere. August air turned concentric comet

tails to burning, locusts came in swarms—and

swarmed—resized the shadows, shallowed soaring from contained electric charge;
they rose, they rise; they bloomed to doom, wakened
serpent holes from cliff rock crevice sliced. They rise]

[White battering perfumes squirm against your hull;
white bludgeoning swirl of harpoon stroke
in dark;
the light, bright white, your eyelids rise]

"I'm sure you shouldn't be texting on those dark
mountain roads," Brad said. His voice echoed
between silhouettes of trees. His fingers reflected
technology; her eyes filled in the tree spots. "Maybe
we will talk soon." He waited. She texted him
the next afternoon:

I should tell you I have a phone phobia. At the very least
I don't like talking on the phone.

[I'd rather sink than call]

80

How many dots did you count in Drowning Girl?

Impossible. 94 in her tears alone, though. Best

I could do.

Describe your experience while counting the dots.

Meditative and frustrating at the same time.

Do the dots remind you of anything?

Monet. Agnes Martin (who I just saw at the Guggenheim). Fluidity

and precision. Trees.[70]

81

Motorcycle George takes photographs of sunlight reflections

on waves in Key West, posts them to his Facebook page. Sometimes

there's a shot of an empty bench, his pedal bike leaned against an upright,

the caption reads, "Another Management Meeting With The Director."

Today, after a meeting, a guy I respect came over and said, 'You fired me up today

Brad.' Thank God, the Director, we don't have to do this thing alone.

---

[70] From a solicited response to *The Drowning Girl Project* sent back via email to Brad & me.

Diamonds, George calls them diamonds, the shimmers and

soaring constructs a lingering sun can make when lounging in long afternoons, or arriving

in the morning, departing at the end of the day. Diamonds, cathedrals made of diamonds.

I can still see Claude Monet making Rouen Cathedral rise, the size of prayers complete like chorus hymns, an artist's subconscious insight

into the universe of the mind. Brad asked for help.

82

Instead of eyes in ears in airport lounges, tie one on,

and let's talk about the things no one ever hears; last chance connections, centers of storms

we look for, measured in miles, the air-to-ground protections standing still in rain welts

cannot guarantee. Lightning on beaches

reaches into stomachs from mouths, southerly, the direction route of un-mailed

missives and hand-scrawled notes, the doubts

of reaching ground from deep water, we hold breaths,[71] exhale,

---

[71] Seen on a bench at the Clark Art Institute: "It can be startling to see someone's breath, let alone the breathing of a crowd. You usually don't believe that people extend that far," a Jenny Holzer truism. When they saw this, Brad said, "Where do I know this from?" He didn't realize he'd seen this at the Walker Art Center on one of his first solo cross-country drives. Back then, before cell phones were affordable, he

and turn our attention

deficits toward grasping hands in need and prayer.
These cathedrals,

these cathedrals, these cathedrals of you and me.
When we visited the ICA in Boston,

Cornelia Parker's charred remains were suspended in a campfire. Somewhere

in the quiet corners a person sipped whiskey today.

Another favorite Jimmy Buffett song:

If The Phone Doesn't Ring, It's Me.

83

The first time Brad visited Montana, his father

held him one morning in the water—the glacial
runoff of Lake McDonald—until his 9-month-old baby

---

feared going mad on stretches of highway by himself. He was old enough to remember ordering maps from AAA. Mergatroid and Brad also used Jenny Holzer marquees for announcements of their first joint art exhibition in 2002. They looked at the bench, Brad and Angela, and talked about the Jenny Holzer projection on the ICA in Boston, the one he'd sent her photos of. This may have been right after the installation Brad and Murgatroid and Bennett performed in. This was after Angela and Brad went to the ICA and he told about his progressive alcoholism underneath a bridge near the Fort Point Channel. It's a Friday at I write this, I'm watching the Red Sox play October baseball, and wondering how long before I read you. The sky above America is baseball lights, homeruns and fouls; everything erupting from the blue-black night.

cheeks shook and turned purple-blue. "What I would
do," his father said, "Was lift you out. And you'd start
to cry. So I'd plop your little ass back down again.

"Your mother finally got after me. 'Take him out,'
she said." A faded photo on the nightstand—part of
Brad's inheritance, showed mountains in reflection; a baptismal
under sky.

84

The painter couldn't make it off of escalators fast enough.
Contained in crowds,
collective gasping had the world spin a few touches faster. Run fast

to catch last-chance elevator rides inside the redesigned
Residence Inn in Midtown and you win immediate confusion. Ducking between

those automatically anatomical doors, a post-kiss
closure collapsing on all sides—anatomically automatic—catches fingertips and skin,
petulant and avoidable. There are no buttons.
Nothing to direct.

True story: There's an elevator in Manhattan without a field

of circular buttons

to press, no telephone keypad to poke and coerce, no Uncle Sam persuasive

landings. Brad got in the elevator and couldn't direct a thing. The elevator

was a camel. The elevator was a donkey. "Maybe,"

a voice said.

85

Angela described herself as intermittent in an email; a rain.

A setting on the windshield wiper knob, twisting opposite of the blinkers, and the flash-

flash preparations for turns. Look down at the directional. Look

down at the other side and twist. Three dots. Three dots; ellipse.

Marquee lights, Morse code, stones around the walkways, you

are here, come home. Jackson Pollock said, "My paintings do not have a center, but depend

on the same amount of interest throughout."[72]

---

[72] *Art News,* May 1951. "Pollock Paints a Picture" by Robert Goodnough

Before he even saw his name in the *Drowning Girl's* gasping mind, Brad posted that note to Facebook along with the photograph his camera phone

took: *Self Portrait In a Lichtenstein (With An Elevator),*

he wrote.

86

His mother lived in a different Plymouth house now than the

one he grew up in.[73] When drinking, Brad wasn't welcome anymore. When sober

a little while, his mother put the house in his name. Brad's mother was a free tenant

in a house he owned and couldn't sell yet. This was a testament to 12 Steps.

One Thanksgiving, they met at Hearth & Kettle inside the

Governor John Bradford Motel for dinner because he wasn't welcome in the home he now owned.

He could still see the terse canyon frown his mother

chewed with embedded

in the terrible Pilgrim and Indian décor.

[73] Overheard at a meeting in South Boston: "I'm lying. I got older there. I'm still working on growing up."

The paintings, and the mother and son; failed relationships

depicted in near-caricature rendering

in a restaurant known for its proximity to historical genocide.

Brad opened one sleepy half eye and looked at Facebook

that morning in Plymouth, Mass. The world rode by on mindless donkeys.[74]

Overheard on a phone call Brad had with Jim Timbre after

Angela's preemptive breakup: "I should be wearing smiley-face slippers. I remember when the Commonwealth of Massachusetts was like, 'I'm sorry,

you're not adult enough for doorknobs.'"

[How many dots in a Lichtenstein?]

[What is Ahab but Cupid with a harpoon?]

87

Brad could remember the glossy hardcover science book

he'd placed beneath a microscope

---

[74] Brad was meditating this morning (10/4) before he found the scorpion in the shower and was reminded of the phrase—Pedal the bike and let God steer. Jack called from Atlanta and said he got lost with Dolly on the way to a meeting. Brad remembered being locked inside a gated sub-development when he had a Palm Pilot, a rental car, and his first GPS plugin. Imagine believing Grandmother Helen's lifeline would be the most extreme.

during a lull in 7th-grade study hall. He remembered reassembling every hotel, motel, amusement park, and
postcard—every Frank O'Hara fire escape drawing, and every interstate
attraction; every Exit Sign—into a single sheet of now. He stepped back and stared into a Lichtenstein. He stared at a
thousand stories beneath a thousand skies, a New York City history, the patterned memories polka-dotting
through his mind.

Of course, Naomi had a place on the Upper East Side
before and after they started dating, dotting. The doorman eventually nodded Brad through and on
and off the elevator (intermittently) until he collaged pieces about these regular arrivals. A series of collections made of gasping. He titled them
"Purple Tulips."

Purple tulips from the deli florist, wrapped in clear plastic
and dripping water droplets from the stems. There are many metaphors for fucking when visiting a florist, many
metaphors for thorns; even Georgia O'Keeffe could shrink away, embarrassed in these openings.

The first time Naomi and Brad kissed, he drove all night from
Carolina, stopped off at outlet stores for better pants and caught himself

bewildered when she said, "Are you coming in?"

at the entry to her bedroom door. Before that,

their lives were only almost; almost perfect

timing, almost lost, and almost found. Throwing off the blankets, an incomplete

Matisse appeared—the flowers shaking, quivering,

and collapsing into vases—falling apart and partially consumed in the space of hours, their

shattering on the nightstand; "I'm almost there," she whispered, her teeth

against his ear, and across the street in evening panes, blinds inclined

and soaring, YOU ARE HERE, he read.

88

Brad's favorite book was *Cat's Cradle* by Kurt Vonnegut:

How this had come about was a mystery. The theoretical

villain, however, was what Dr. Breed called "a seed."

He meant by that a tiny grain of the undesired crystal pattern.

The seed, which had come from God-only-knows-where, taught

the atoms the novel way in which to stack and lock, to crystallize,

to freeze. "Now think about cannonballs on a courthouse lawn

or about oranges in a crate again," he suggested. And he helped

me to see that the pattern of the bottom layers of cannonballs
or of oranges determined how each subsequent layer would stack
and lock. "The bottom layer is the seed of how every cannonball
or every orange that comes after is going to behave, even to an
infinite number of cannonballs or oranges."

89

Brad, the former artist, hesitated at the thought of elevators and
feared airplanes like the plague. The reason Brad was
only a former artist, and not a current one, was he couldn't even
paint a Tinder profile portrait. Smack dab
in the most attractive
spot in America, he didn't know where to start: My
parents, My art, My Boston accent, My consulting business, My
traveling, My pivotal moment
inside the Whitney when I caught Mark Rothko's
retrospective: I looked inside
the blue, inside the black behind, and knew
what the end of the movie was.

Tag line for a Tinder profile page: Was I riding a Rumi donkey
or a Buddha horse this entire time? It's crazy here in
terms of storms.

By here, I mean this multiverse. By here, I mean my mind.

90

Brad looked up from his train seat. He wrote the words,
A Timeline.

Kalispell, MT, my father's father, leaves.
Kalispell, MT, my father joins the army at age 14.
My parents meet in a bar. My father offers to knock out the
guys harassing my mom.

My mother is almost 6 months pregnant before she knows.

They treat her
for shock.

My father is sober 6 months when my mother asks
for a divorce. There are back-of-matchbook stories and
girls looking

wide-eyed at my father's Montana Sky eyes beforehand.
Never write anything down, he says. Look
at the numbers scrawled.

91

Brad looked up from his bus seat. He wrote the words,

A Timeline.

[I leave Key West on 9/15, stay overnight in Miami.

I leave Miami, stay overnight on the train.

I arrive in New York; the Chelsea pipe bomb

goes off. I stay

overnight 10 blocks away.

I take the bus to Boston. I take the Commuter Rail to Plymouth, stay overnight twice.

I drive to Western Mass

and Adams. Angela thinks

I'm staying over. Instead, I sleep at a Holiday Inn close enough to the MoCA

to see silver carve the sign.[75] I drive back to Plymouth,

---

[75] This is not a metaphor or a reference to an Ace of Base song. 10/6/2016 after coffee with another Lisa—another Lisa, a Key West Lisa (Lisa's abound)—she Facebook messages me. I'm still having trouble with my cell phone and she's still having trouble with her marriage. "Is Ace of Base a reference you understand?" she asks. "Or is this more problems with our generation gap?" I'm driving past the church Hemingway paid penance to on Sundays after becoming a Teabag Catholic.* Today (10/7) I walked by a sign on Whitehead Street nearly hidden in a flower bush. "Hemingway Pissed Here" it said. The first Angela I ever kissed; sometime before I met her, I got arrested at her house. The first short story I ever wrote in a college

I stop

at Herman Melville's house,[76]

I go back to Plymouth. I take the Commuter Rail to Boston, hit

The Noonie. I see Georgie B and Doug "The Deal" Coyle. Me and George

go to the projects and see the center he built for local kids. My paintings hang

there. My paintings are hanged.

That weekend I go to Stonehill College on retreat. I think of

Angela. I see Mickey and Rembrandt's *Prodigal Son* reproduced in poster form. I spend time with D-Mac

---

level workshop for Melinda Haystacks at Syracuse University was about that First Angela night, my first arrest, the first time I stopped drinking for the rest of my life. I got the announcement for a painting contest today and clicked right on a picture of your ex. Angela the First's future ex was my best friend. The night I got arrested he put me in a headlock a number of times to stop me from driving away and dying in a horrific car crash. I repaid him in arm bite marks and lumps around his skull from punching. When I arrived in Alcoholics Anonymous I nearly treated all those old timers in the exact same way. Try and save me and I'll try and kill you. Love me and I leave. (*"Teabag Catholics" pray only when they're in hot water).

[76] I'm talking to Dolly on the phone and stop. Melville thought Greylock looked like a whale emerging? But Greylock was my grandma's *Moby Dick*. Greylock was my grandpa's *Moby Dick*. In both cases I mean the whale. Mark Twain and Melville both began with catastrophic shipwrecks. Catastrophic firsts are starting points. What we appropriate from books is unexplainable. A pipe bomb just went off.

and Two Chance. I tell Francis Donavan after

in a Facebook message that I ate more pancakes without him there but missed him regardless. Mark Connolly couldn't come because he just got out of the hospital. I spend Sunday and Monday with my mom. Eat dinner

with Jonny Mac Sunday night and see a guy at a Marshfield[77] meeting I saw in Key West a few weeks back.

92

The world is small, but I wouldn't want to paint it.[78]

That Tuesday

Brad went in town,[79] had coffee with Lisa Montague, his sponsor Eddie too, hit a meeting at Arch Street, had lunch

---

[77] Brad lived in Marshfield with the Swillz brothers in '94 when he quit Syracuse and didn't go back after getting pinched for possession with intent to distribute. This was years after he wore their old and ill-fitting clothes.

[78] See the Sherwin Williams ad with enamel paint covering the world. It's bizarre enough to give you goosebumps. It's a Ben Day dot painted over. It's a wound hole from a harpoon. It's an exit sign.

[79] Locally we call going into Boston "Going in town." And we call Manhattan "The City." Brad wore a Red Sox hat in the rain his entire second stint in NYC this time. Fuck the Yankees.

with Chuckie Klimt and Jim Timbre, walked

down and caught the Ai WeiWei *Zodiac Heads* near the old Customs Tower, walked back to South Station and had coffee with Francis Suspin,

had dinner with Jack and Dolly at South Station and headed back.

His mother picked him up at the train station. Her

lateness brought anxiety from back when she'd pass out when

Brad was in High School and not grab him

at the drop-off after basketball away games. She got out of the

car with her cane and asked him to drive. Not because she was drunk now—she never admitted

to being drunk—she quit drinking. Instead, she has these cataracts. Time is a fucking trip.

Time is Braille dots for the deaf; orchestras for the blind. God

owns the future and the past. If you go there, just know you're trespassing.

On Thursday, Brad took the train to Boston, the bus to Manhattan, and stayed over.

I went to MoMA.

Brad stayed over again. Left on Sunday on the train for Miami

and stayed over

on the train. Brad ended up in Miami Beach, stayed over, took the bus to Key West and arrived on 10/3. That's two weeks. That's 40-plus years before.

There was a note in his post office box when I returned. Brad replied with a manifesto.

93

After however long on Cape Cod, failed Saab Dealership and all, Kurt Vonnegut said he felt at home in Manhattan, or Skyscraper National Park, as he called it. Brad called Vonnegut his Uncle Kurt to anyone who would listen.

On Facebook, he shared updates, *Uncle Kurt,* he wrote. Once, Naomi got tickets to see KV in Harvard Square. Once, Naomi went to a reading in Manhattan, and the father of Kilgore Trout scrawled an autograph on the inside cover of *Cat's Cradle.*

He made some Pall Mall-tinged comment about her not buying the newest book. Kurt Vonnegut was so alive then.

Naomi and Brad dated off and on for 6 years. A lovely and beautiful girl, the last time Brad saw her was five years after they broke up, and walked separate ways out of a counselor's office in Government Center near the coffee pot that steamed. He'd said to her six months earlier: Let's go. Counseling can either teach us how to stay together or teach us how to stay apart. That counselor, who looked quite similar to the Cuban Catholic lady who does Brad's wash and fold in Key West certainly earned her copay.

94

They hadn't seen or heard from each other in five years, the day Brad walked to Park Street Church for the 5:30 meeting. He never went to that meeting, hardly ever, but that day he handed someone a check for 70,000 dollars, sort of shaking. He made phone calls, pacing in empty artist loft space, and caught someone on their way in town. He checked the round clock face. He paced and stopped and checked the clock again. "I'm on my way," he said.

Nervous energy dissipated in trains bolting down through Chinatown, edging the old Combat Zone, through Downtown

Crossing, past the Public Gardens. Almost there, bolting to try and find a seat. At the top of one of the subway staircases, a girl looked straight at him. "Brad," she said.

He kept walking. "Brad?"

He stopped. It was Naomi.

95

Up until then, Brad had this joke, gallows humor. He'd see a girl with long blonde hair walking downtown, turn to Greenback, and say, “Hey Naomi.” Brad imagined his insides as a World Trade Center tower. Seeing her would be an airplane.

96

Brad gave her a hug. “Naomi!”

“What have you been up to?” she said. “I just bought a house. A condo. Today, I just, just now, bought a loft.” “Are you still living in Fort Point?[80]”

He was.

“Great area. Where was all that money when we were dating?”

“That’s what happens when you date someone who’s two seconds sober.”

She laughed, wide-mouthed and elegant. “Back then,” he said.

“I know I did a lot of hurtful things. I hope you will forgive me. When I think of you, I only think good things.”Brad didn’t remember what she said next with an air of dismissive grace.

---

[80] I cannot tell you how big Brad smiled later when he realized Naomi had been keeping tabs.

He rubbed her shoulder in circles.

"Hey," she said, a man approaching. "Brad, this is my husband, Charles." Tall, dark, and handsome walking; the man Brad pictured Naomi married to before the church bell rang. They shook his hands to 5:30, now ringing. "That's my meeting," Brad said. "I gotta go."

The last-last time he ever saw Naomi.

97

Itinerary: Get out of that Key West gym. Listen to Sara Bareilles on the road at least (no exaggeration) 100 times. Have

Barbara drop him off at the bus station next to the airport where colored murals read: *Conch Republic.* Greyhound

to Miami. Uber to Little River Club for a meeting.[81] They laughed when Brad came clean

---

[81] One of the stupidest things Brad ever did in over twenty years of 12 Step meetings: he took an Uber to the Little River Club in Miami using GPS. They got there, and the building wasn't familiar. He told the guy, "This isn't right," and looked it up again online. Had him take Brad 15 minutes away to the address he'd found. Only this was the old address. They'd moved since last Brad visited. He had to have him take Brad all the back to the first place in Little Haiti. Was Brad the only one who thinks of Miami Vice whenever he hit town? Whenever Brad's father saw a limousine he'd say, "Lookie there, Bradley, It's Don Johnson." Incidentally, Brad caught alcoholism from a toilet seat in Plymouth, Mass in 1987.

on his sober dyslexia. He also suffered from sober blackouts.)

Go back: Watching *Girls* in Key West, there was a Kiss/Ace

Frehley song, "New York Groove" to end it all. To prepare to start again. The KISS in white strobe lights.

Go Back: Brad's first field trip with Francis Suspin, Brad

stormed off the bus

and called her. Suspin said, "Brad, if anything's this difficult, it's just not

meant to be."

Go forward: Brad took another Uber to the train station—a kid

from Massachusetts who started chewing OC's in Fall River drove for the company and seemed

embarrassed when Brad insisted on paying. Brad insisted on praying and handed

the boy a business card.[82]

Brad took the train from Miami to New York, stayed only one night in Manhattan—

---

[82] Someday, or some painting, Brad promised to tell you about all his friends who've died from drug and alcohol addiction. He thought of painting a series titled *Veterans of Domestic Wars*. He was in a meeting on 42nd Street last night and a woman from Indianapolis who was 8 years sober said "I am going to cure alcoholism." Brad couldn't tell if it was a tribute or an insult to every single life we've lost.

the night the latest bomb went off in Chelsea. He took the bus to Boston

and then the commuter rail to Plymouth, Mass. Brad's mother picked him up

in her old lady Cadillac.

He drove out to Western Mass, visited his grandparent's grave. He took photos of their old family home in Cheshire. He forgot his still- alive mother had a headstone there. She wrote her name, Brad knew, as insurance against another marriage.

Brad and Angela went to The Clark. Had dinner. Brad thought, I almost stayed

at your place until this very moment.

98

The reason for some variation of NAME, OCCUPATION, SITUATION,

as a possible opener is the power of the first lines in every Elmore Leonard novel

from his prime.

Elmore "Dutch" Leonard, the most unsung literary master of the American 20th Century

could suck you into a story in three beats or less. Check the opening line of *Tishomingo Blues*:

Dennis Lenahan the high diver would tell people that if you put a fifty-cent piece

on the floor and looked down at it, that's what the tank looked like from the top

of that eighty-foot steel ladder.

Check *Glitz*:

The night Vincent was shot, he saw it coming.

Brad returned to books like old friends. He associated books with places.

He went to reunions. He recommended books when people

took trips. As a rule, Brad loved books and paintings more than people. [Now go back and reread

that Dutch Master Music. Count yourself the blue notes] Elmore Leonard for Miami. (*La Brava*)

Pat Conroy, Charleston, SC. (*Beach Music* and everything)

Elmore Leonard and casinos. Every time Brad walked in

a casino he thought of *Glitz*)

Elmore Leonard owned Detroit. (Brad couldn't go to the RenCen without thinking about Clooney and J-Lo).

Raymond Chandler, LA.
Jack London, Oakland.
Mark Twain, Lake Tahoe.
Frank O'Hara, New York City.
Jonathan Lethem, Brooklyn (*Motherless Brooklyn, The Fortress of Solitude*).
John D. MacDonald, Ft. Lauderdale & Sarasota
Nathaniel Philbrick, Nantucket

Whales. Whales. Whales.

99

Key West lumps in everybody: Hem, Vonnegut, Frost. Although there's

a darkness and death in winter in New England Brad
associated with Frost's

poems, and some of the landscape paintings of Alex Katz.

Dutch also said never start with the weather. There's a hurricane on its way.

100

A YouTube clip titled *The Towering Inferno:*

Scenic Elevator Explosion,
as there can be nothing so terrifying as a single dot separating
from gravity and magnetized toward the ground until a
second before a second circular shadow appears.

Our ears disappear, the sear of silence
bounces off empty. These falls are stain-glassed
and on the verge of becoming shards. Just as during Brad's visit
to the Rothko Retrospective at The Whitney he knew
the painter captured moments between light-catching color
and light catching ground. Catapulting off the fire
prayers, a pressing together of heat and night, a single body
becoming the sun, or moon, or the history
of descent. The single dot becomes Nostradamus; a 9/11
prophecy.

What do you remember most about New York? What
do you forget?

101

Mr. and Mrs. Smith: Angelina's hitmen colleagues cut the wires
on an elevator holding Brad in an attempt to kill him.
Not a movie, but an urban legend that might be true: a friend
of my cousin
got into an elevator in New York and went up a few

floors. Bill Murray got on.

When they got to my cousin's friend's floor, Bill Murray stared over and said,

"No one will ever believe you."

Jerry Maguire. How can you not love a movie
about someone taking a chance?
Goldfish and all.

Roy Lichtenstein drove over that bridge en route from suburban New Brunswick, New Jersey to urban Manhattan amid the realities of 1961 America, something inescapable when confronting nearly all of the pictures here.

Newly elected JFK, the first Intercontinental Ballistic Missile tests, the first man in space (Russian), Adolf Eichmann's Nazi War Crimes Trial in Jerusalem, the second man in space (American), Freedom Riders & Civil Rights Movement, The Bay of Pigs. JFK was urging civilians to build fallout shelters; the construction of the Berlin Wall commenced. The promise and consumption of a victorious America, savior of the free world during World War II, had become an anxious weight as the Cold War escalated into suburbia.

The world hadn't only changed from the promise of free expression in the hands of the Abstract Expressionist with the shifting center of the art world from Paris to New York; in 1961, the technology that had promised utopia now seemed poised to deliver apocalypse.

103

Ryan Grater says a strainer, and Jennifer says triangles. I say one of those boards
you hang in a garage to put tools on.
A Light Bright board; candy dots (the candy *Dots*); molecules;
Band-Aids[83] with black paint in the little holes; God particles, every one of us,
measured in the extending outposts of far-reaching technology, magnetized marvelously and sewn together with
trailing rope, balanced

in the approaching storm's eye; the receiver of a phone; the
mouthpiece—thumbtacks, fish eggs, a thimble side (the kind Brad's grandmother protected her thumbs with). A sheet
of Bubble Wrap packaging with air pockets,
beads she'd pop, cracking every single one with twists. Plastic
six-pack carrying rings before we realized convenience came in seagull doom.

[Looks like my screen has a bunch of holes in it]

---

[83] Band-Aids are a registered brand of Johnson & Johnson.

At the start of the video from 1959, Dodie Stevens gets prepped on the corded phone before singing into the mouthpiece. Every phone, so jet black then; every number dialed a hay-stacked mile piled high on the sides of fields plowed bright to dotted white. She sings:

He wears tan shoes with pink shoelaces
A polka dot vest and man, oh, man
Tan shoes with pink shoelaces
And a big Panama with a purple hat band
Ooh-ooh, ooh, ooh
Ooh-ooh, ooh, ooh

[ELEVATOR MUSIC]

He takes me deep-sea fishing in a submarine
We got to drive-in movies in a limousine
He's got a whirly-birdy and a 12-foot yacht
Ah, but that's-a not all he's got
He's got tan shoes with pink shoelaces
A polka dot vest and man, oh, man
Tan shoes with pink shoelaces
And a big Panama with a purple hat band

[ELEVATOR MUSIC]

Also, my bathroom floor. Those awful nylon shorts & tanks we had as kids that were made from the fabric full

of holes. A flashback to 1977 and polyester fashion. More
popping with popcorn kernels prepped
this time. And one of those metal things you stick your face in
at the *Sharper Image.* The outline remains. There are
ripples in a stream, tears,
or rocks, or binary drowning, always.

On *LinkedIn,* Brad wrote messages to former employers.
Benjamin Griddle wrote back, *Hang in There.*
[The light you see might just be
the end of the tunnel and not an approaching train]

[But even if you're on the right track
eventually, you will get run the fuck over
if you stay still]

Now Dooley had a feelin' we were goin' to war
So he went out and enlisted in a fightin' corps
But he landed in the brig for raisin' such a storm
When they tried to put 'em in a uniform
He wanted tan shoes with pink shoelaces
A polka dot vest and man, oh, man
He wanted tan shoes with pink shoelaces
And a big Panama with a purple hat band
Ooh-ooh, ooh, ooh
Ooh-ooh, ooh, ooh

[ELEVATOR SILENCES; ELEVATOR PRAYERS]
[LOOK UP]

Brad's mother had that phrase on an '80s poster in her
basement bindery: A cat, clutching on for dear life to a branch. *Hang In There,*
it said.
Brad entered the phrase "Damien Hirst dots and skulls"
in Google Image Search (the best painting assistant
in America): Wonder Bread costumes, patterns
of a storm, butterflies, and sharks.

104

Brad's counselor told him, and this was after Naomi left,
to learn to lean in and wait. Hold your hand
(supporting open blue) wide open, be true, and let the butterfly land, let the butterfly come to you. And sharks.
Butterflies and sharks. Above and below, there are tracking mechanisms, arrows and hash marks, bottles dotted
with red messages across ocean into horizon, a hundred horizons, a million faces
upturned to light. Delight, stare back
in crinkled eye corners,
a thousand more faces of God.

[YOU ARE HERE]

One train may hide another like black hides black on black.

105

Is Brad and Angelina's split the only time a couple's
separation has eradicated a word? Forget the kids.
What happens to the word “Brangelina” now? Does it morph
into an adjective for elegant romantic despair? Does Webster’s hit delete?

Who was it that said intimacy was like standing out on a limb
and handing someone a saw?

Us Weekly[84] says: *Inside Brad’s Shattered World. Missing his kids*
and reeling from heartbreak, Pitt tries
to put his life back together as nasty rumors swirl.

Drowning Girl says *I’d rather sink than call.*

---

[84] October 17, 2016.

106

The Ben-Day dots printing process, named after illustrator

and printer Benjamin Henry Day, Jr., (son of 19th Century publisher Benjamin Henry Day)

is a technique dating from 1879.[85]

Herman Melville's *Moby Dick* was published

on October 18, 1851. Coincidentally, Brad changed his Facebook profile pic

to a portrait of Arrowhead's most famous

resident just the other day.

107

Start at the Ground. Stare at the ground. Maybe once or twice, critics could be right, as with Bennett Murgatroid's observation of artworks; There are so many shoes, Brad. There are so many shoes. Call this inheritance. Brad's father was abandoned by his father, then abandoned by his mother. In our family, *Missoula* means something sacred and hidden you hold your boy away from your chest for. *Sonny,* she called him. *Sonny,* she called me.

Our hairs were both so white back then. Start with Grandma Linda on a horse farm up the Rattlesnake. The first time Brad

---

[85] Courtesy of Wikipedia.

drove cross-country under one year old he rode in a crib in the back seat and stood up the entire trip.

Only thing anyone on the internet wanted to talk about was what Hurricane Matthew was about to do to Haiti. Brad was on his way to get on the bus and go back to Key West

There are no footprints on the train. Depending on the gods

you pray to.

108

The hurricane tracks have the models moving west toward the
Southernmost Point tonight. A Tropical
Storm Warning may be issued for parts
of the Florida Keys
tomorrow. I told you I should have stayed.

109

Hurricane Translators: Have I mentioned yet? Matthew
is on his way in the background of this poem, listening
to *The Scorpions* in his headphones.

But Elmore Leonard said to never start with the weather.

By the way, this is a poem

about art,[86] but Elmore Leonard is art. Probably one of the greatest writers of the 20th Century. He could start a novel with a sentence[87] and immediately suck you in.

An aside: We can lose track of our disasters.

110

On the way to New York:

---

[86] This is not a poem about art. If I were doing footnotes on my footnotes I'd start to count the lies. In 9th Grade in Ms. Eastwoods's class she said the theme of *The Great Gatsby* was the American Dream. I was never a big fan of drawing attention to myself, even though I always wanted more attention. "Everyone get it?" she said. "Umm," I said, "I think the theme is love." There was a larger dialogue in the class about how Gatsby wanted love. Did he want love? What is love? No one was swayed. Me against the world. Someone should have walked me to a rake laying on the lawn and said "Step on this a couple hundred times right now kid because the world is going to mangle you." When you misunderstand gaping, bottomless need, and the greed that turns innocent love into possession in the 9th Grade you will still be unmarried by age 42. A Pirate Looks at 42. Alternative first line for *The Great Gatsby*, "She had legs like white picket fences and a mouth as puffy as suburban lawns." If there are archetypes of literature, as well as the human psyche/experience, as there surely are, then Scott Fitzgerald created a new one with Gatsby. America created a new one with Capitalism. Getting what you want will fuck you over and such. In the 3-D movie version I loved the snow. The snow.

[87] Every novel starts with a sentence. I am indicating the quality of his sentences not the use of them in general.

In the gym in Key West, where another girl named Sara,[88] besides the Bareilles, this one a weightlifter, approached Brad on some random pre-New York day. She smiled and said he must be from the northeast because of all his t-shirts. Brad couldn't tell if she was flirting or trying to sell personal training.

He looked down.

From Nashua, New Hampshire, she corrected Brad when he said "Nash Vegas."

"That's Manch-Vegas," she said.

His attempt at Rickles[89] came when she said, "I'm actually from

---

[88] I fell in lust with a girl named Sarah when I was in middle school and listened to the song by *Starship*, recorded from FM radio in cassette tape, a half a million times. Stereos should come with Braille odometers.

[89] Brad's father loved Don Rickles. When Brad played t-ball, a game he thought ridiculous, he played for the Dodgers. Their hats were '80s powder blue puffy hats with white plastic mesh and snap back and an iron-on D on front. Don Rickles used to call people "Dummy." His comedy album is titled "Hello Dummy." In a riff on Johnny Carson, Brad's father said, "And Heeeeeeerrrrre's Dummy," whenever Brad wore that Dodger's hat. He called it Brad's Dummy hat. "Go get your Dummy hat, Brad." Brad's father was also stellar at baseball. His father, who left when Brad's dad was tiny, was a manager for professional baseball teams in Montana. The grandfather Brad never met, who looked like an aging Humphrey Bogart in photos Brad later saw, got lambasted by *The Daily Interlake* for his non-segregated management. Brad's father played baseball and shot pool lefty because

New Hampshire," and he said, "I'm sorry."

Key West gyms are super tight pants and impossible fitness clothes. Her legs were bigger than Brad's, muscular and thick and ready for the business of cracking walnuts or watermelons; or the heads of male and female wrestlers on Pay-Per-View TV specials produced by Vince McMahon.

Brad decided after all that dieting and lifting weights, all the time on the elliptical, (the ellipsis-forming elliptical with tracking numbers made in red light dots) this slender version of himself made it more probable she was flirting. Flirting in the gym.

In the past, when women looked at Brad in the gym, he knew it was because he was using one of the machines wrong.

[I'm leaving New York now and regret the two cookies I bought at the train station]

If you're lost, so am I. At some point, I'll plot points and dates like forecasters retracing their predictions. The weatherman ruined my life. At the start

of every weather forecast should be a recap of yesterday's attempt at accuracy.

---

his right eye was so much better than his left.

111

Start Spreading The News, Brad's father would sing. *I'm Leaving Today*. Brad's bestest family heirloom was the cassette tape his stepmother found

after Dad passed. On one side, he and Brad sing—a freshly divorced version of him, a 4-year-old version of Brad.

On the other side, a possibly drunk reversion

of him croons like Frank Sinatra. Time is a cassette tape that's been redubbed and copied,

shared; a cassette tape that's lifted moments from the radio, been flipped over

and re-erased.

Overheard at a meeting: It's always 3 AM

in the heart of an alcoholic.

112

The elevators, in their post-yawn return, all of them:

You'll find no buttons

for pressing, no nervous habits to redirect. At the

Renaissance Inn

in Midtown Manhattan, now there are no buttons

in the elevator at all. Navigate

the lobby touchscreen, and a computer tells you where to go. CLICK[90],

Brad took a picture of the YOU ARE HERE plaque glued

against the wall.

His new version of landscape painting combines words, red dots, and EXIT signs.

A joke from 12 Step meetings: "I'm not going to say much. Okay, my parents met…."

Another: "Where should I start? Okay, I'll start at the

beginning."

Where is anyone in the world without being on their way to New York City?[91]

Brad, on the way: He listens to Sara Bareilles sing *Manhattan* again

and again and again.[92]

---

[90] There was absolutely not a clicking sound.

[91] Hannah is in a cab listening to Kiss/Ace Frehley do "New York Groove." That song is made abundantly better by the editing and production team on the show, and by the context of Lena Dunham. How can someone have a character say early on in the series, ironically "I think I'm the voice of my generation" and then become it?

[92] Jim Timbre said to Brad on retreat: "I'll listen to a song until I'm

[I miss my dad.[93] But I never wish he was still alive. He was in so much fucking pain]

113

There are so many bridges to nowhere. The Overseas Highway; sad the train

can't happen on this bridge. And has there ever been a painter who looked

through a spot in a broken bridge and saw just

a broken bridge?

---

sick of it."

[93] Two times Brad knew his father went to New York City: 1) He went to Tavern on the Green after always hearing about it, and thinking it had to be the fanciest and most elegant place in America. He was disappointed. 2) When Naomi and Brad started dating, his dead father visited her in her dreams. He crept around her apartment on East 93rd and told her not to screw around with his son. On a separate note, like Brad's Grandfather Red (Brad's mother's father), Brad's father loved the ocean. He loved Cape Cod and full-bellied fried clams. He liked to sit and eat from paper clam boats, dunk full bellies into tartar sauce and ask the person closest by, "You ever eat Rocky Mountain Oysters?" When he said Oysters, he said Ersters. All of life is a duet between Lois Armstrong and Ella Fitzgerald.

114

From Google:[94]

noun: **poem**; plural noun: **poems**

1. a piece of writing that partakes of the nature
   of both speech
   and song that is nearly always rhythmical,
   usually metaphorical,
   and often exhibits such formal elements
   as meter, rhyme,
   and stanzaic structure.

   synonyms: verse, rhyme, piece of poetry, song
   "Lydia saved every poem that Marshall
   wrote that year."

   - Something that arouses strong emotions because of its beauty. "you make a poem
     of riding downhill on your bike."

---

[94] Soon we will have to always give a where and a when. To misquote Einstein on the universe: "Shit is getting crazy." The idea that we are possible projections from a larger force is a chicken and egg question. What's crossing the street? Here in Key West, it's an angry mob of roosters. They congregate near the Stop Light at White Street and Truman—the extra-long traffic signal—and inhale the fumes of their brothers and sisters frying with potato wedges.

115

Brad's father always said:

"Women are like buses. There's another one coming in 10 minutes. Just wait."

116

Jasper Johns loves/loved birds: "The barn sheltered his collection

of guinea fowl. The birds, he explains, had 'disappeared. One was run over.

A few were eaten by fox or coyote or whatever we have up here.' They're particularly

stupid, in his view, but he was fond of them nonetheless. 'They made horrible

sounds, which I love. They were beautiful birds.'"[95]

---

[95] "Jasper Johns: 'Regrets belong to everybody, don't they?'" a piece written by Julie L Belcove, published by The Financial Times on February 14, 2014 (Valentine's Day), on the occasion of Johns' (then) upcoming exhibition at MoMA. I asked myself tonight. Will these connected/separate dots ever think to end? Cupid firing arrow holes in rapid, insistent response.

117

Dear Angela:

I meant it about the killers. Your people get Adirondack
slats; mine stand in line for electric. Everything is
chairs.

Before I left Key West, the dinner girl spoke;
She'd counted to 57 between her patio and parlor. You
mentioned a lake. A big blue lake, before
you admitted to phone line phobias.
How can we pray through all those telephone pole
Jesus pieces if you can't pick up the phone?

I promised my mother I'd take her out shopping
for a chair. In the hierarchy of distances and desire,
texts and phones and Facebook Messenger,
smartphone apps, and Skype descends.

What stars reflect inside your eyes
tonight, too startled to blink or rotate? What starts
these constellations? Every culture traces hope
against hope against distances. This equation: Which
direction will the time-lapse trace, each proof of leaving

a strain or scratch against film spool exposure; where
else can I change the view, lay down, and do
the looking?

118

A lesson about love and words:
My father stopped off at *McGrath's*
before the Blizzard of '78 arrived.

Don't forget the genealogy of music and this type
of traveling. Record grooves and tracks. At Penn
Station, a beehive of humanity stared up for a sign. Track 1,
Track 18, Track 8, Track 9, all the way down low

to Miami. When I drive through Miami, I listen to the live
version of Counting Crows and scream the line
"Come on bahhhhbveeeeee, come on bahhhaeeehbee" while
thumping hand fat
on the steering wheel top.
It makes me incredibly
nostalgic in the rearview. I lost count this trip of all
my elevator rides.

119

If everybody loves New York City so much,
why do we keep blowing it up on film?
Is this Hollywood
subconsciously competing with traditional views of theater in America?
Is this 9/11 on repeat from the hidden terrorized cells
of our separate and individual hair follicles and fingernails, wisdom teeth
and tongues, the crevices of eyelids, footpads, knee backs, and genitalia? Are we projecting an explosion
whenever we unfurl a green screen flag? What happened
in the latest superhero movie? New York City blew up. What happened in the latest indie
romantic dramedy? Here we were again, stuck
at the end of the world.

These are the keywords you will hear
when it comes to Hurricane Matthew:
Cone, model, track;
Cone, model, track.
On the news, on Facebook, and everywhere;
Cone, model, track.

Technology means we know less in brighter colors.
Cone, model, track.

120

New York Memories:

Lingering jet lag, the kind for conjuring clouds in pillowcase
indentations—of thunderstorm hair beyond any
snooze alarm
remedies concocted in the afternoons—plagued my two-bedroom
in the South Hills of Missoula past my second-year return and followed me into the new semester. Across the room

I placed the same
digital clock once set for 4:30 am on Christmas morning[96] in 1987,
when equal parts fallout shelter air horn and mechanical unreasoning robot shriek takeover pushed my father up from the pullout couch to groan, "Gee-sus
Key-riced. Turn that fucking thing off." In Montana, I crossed the room,
collapsed back into bed, near-horizontal before my landings. At one point

[96] Evidence of Brad's father's sainthood: After he got sober, he came and stayed with them at Christmas every year. He went back to his old house and his old friends and his old in-laws and his imbibing ex-wife and never said an un-Christmas-like word.

that late summer/fall, I almost broke my neck

in a historical alarm tag injury.

Phone ringing and ringing that morning. Phone ringing

and alarm ringing and phone ringing; alarm. Ryan

Grater on the other end. "Brad," he said. "Are you awake? Do you know

what's going on?"

"Turn on the TV," he said. "They all took off

from Boston." (2001)

121

When Brad told Murgatroid about his evolving fear of airplanes

and the pending trip to San Francisco three weeks after 9/11, his fear of losing Naomi in the aftermath of a national disaster greater than his fear of falling seven miles and having the recurring

thought for the next infinite years of infinity-plus-one echoing through

his dark matter in the after-after life:

"I never should have agreed to fly."

"I've been reading through black box

transcripts," Murgatroid

said the night before Brad's departure.
"They're pretty interesting."

I don't think Brad responded. He and I saw those people in the
video hold hands and plummet from the side of the
World Trade Center.

Wondering to ourselves: burning.
He thought, burning. I thought;
burning. How can burning be worse
than all that empty space careening?

122

"Sometimes it's crazy. The pilot says something like, 'Can I have an orange juice?'
and that's it. Also, you know how they say you just have a heart attack
and die before you hit the ground?"

Brad said a "Yes," Murgatroid laughed at the tone of. "I guess that isn't true," he said.
"If you think about terminal velocity, and you're all those miles in air.
It takes some time to make it to the ground."

123

Quizony.com on a Saturday night:

What famous artist should have painted your portrait? (29 questions)

In the multiple choices of every single question set

Brad's first answer selection was never available.

124

Depending on your viewpoint, everything in America either starts or ends

at Plymouth Rock.[97] Brad started ending there.

He woke up the Monday

before he was supposed to head back to Key West and Hurricane Translators abounded.

---

[97] My High School Yearbook was called *The Rock.* When I worked as a Camp Counselor and Outdoor Education Instructor, Joe Oldman would wait until the Japanese tourists, 35mm cameras hanging from their necks, got close enough. Then he would say, "Do you see the pink haze on the quartz there?" pretending to be talking to the students, but loud enough for eavesdropping. "That's where they couldn't remove the blood stains. The Pilgrims murdered Indians there, used a hatchet against their necks." Gulp.

Sean Mac, the comedian, NOAA, Facebook; Brad's friends

who lived in The Keys forever could be in the middle of a hurricane and say,

"it's not that bad." But he was due to take a train to Miami and a bus

to the Southernmost Point. There were words like model, cone, and track beginning to dull in repetition, already, and Matthew filling screens. Brad's first

thought was, Maybe I don't have to go back. Second was, Angela's letter

will be lost in a deluge.

Kurt Vonnegut was not Brad's uncle or mine either.

But I was named

after my Grandmother Helen's favorite uncle. No one had ever heard of Frank Sinatra when my father was born in Kalispell, Montana,

but during his entire adult life, he felt a kinship with Old Blue Eyes. My father

drank Jack Daniels and played craps. He sang like a champ and became

the center of any room he ever occupied. My father loved Jack Kennedy

and had a framed 3 by 5 feet photograph in his office of JFK. His entire life,

if Francis Albert Sinatra held a pair of Jacks, my father

held the other two.[98]

In every biography there is a family tree.

If you shake my family tree,
milk cartons covered in missing persons
come out.

Empty bottles
come tumbling down.

125

More from the September 30 Rumi (*A Trace*):

> People ask, Which roof is your roof?
> I answer, Wherever the soul came from
> and wherever it goes back to at night,
> my roof[99] is in that direction.

---

[98] The angriest my father ever got with me fell into the category of silent scorn. We were playing poker by a campfire in Upstate New York, using slippery disk poker chips. I laughed and explained I'd been cheating, He quietly put the cards in the box, put the red chips in a plastic bag, and told me it was bedtime.

[99] A Gorky Google search reveals *Goats on the Roof* to be the title of a collection of his letters. I wonder if I own this book, in storage,

126

Brad’s mother bought him a car for 50 bucks to drive to

meetings so he could take the job back at camp. He never knew if it would start, and you

could take the key out and let her run, shock absorbers warped and coasting chassis.

The double-CD Wu-Tang album, fresh out, attached to tape deck, and Sony

Discman, we had a place to stay since Emma’s uncle worked

for AP.

Out the window that night, the Empire State Building

stared back

at our naked bodies moving. Moving lights and bass thumps of innards

twisting as the rhyming innuendos of summer heat and traffic

---

somewhere. The Google Search “Goats on the Roof Gorky [redacted]” came back “Your search - *arshile gorky goats on the roof [redacted]* - did not match any documents.” I wasn’t sure if I blogged about it, or if an early version of me blogged about it. Google is a God to some. Google is my memory. I think “Goats on the Roof” refers to both an architectural nightmare for the residents of Armenia, where Gorky emigrated from, as well as a euphemism for crazy thoughts. Squirrels in the attic. One of my favorite stories about Gorky is when he was desperate to escape the upcoming draft of WW2. He wrote to the government, offering his services as a camouflage painter. See Warhol later. See Gorky.

had the two of us

crashing into bedsprings, clutching hold of sweaty edges, knowing our chance

for loving us had refolded into mornings when concentrated on making linens

into box shapes, we carefully put our other selves

away. (1996)

Rothko at The Whitney (1999).

Naomi's roommates were gone someplace

on summer weekends

and Brad arrived to find a red wraparound skirt

decorated with Caribbean fish and tasseled edges,

the batting threads

thick and wobbly in candlelit sways of hello

and longer hellos.

Blonde and Connecticut, her family a Fairfield Porter lawn,

Naomi's connection to Erykah Badu

couldn't seem innate

without factoring her sensuality, those plump pink lips,

green ocean

eyes—all of them and us (the two of us) breathing

from someplace else. Sway, baby, sway, until bodies are music

and the dinner might have to wait. Sometime soon the

Puerto Rican Day

Parade sounds, steel horns, car horns, and undulating eager throbbing pumps

        of humanity urging on past

woke me late in the weekend morning after making love again and again.

        I could never live in New York, I said that day. (1998)

127

Me in Chelsea, and the bomb goes off. Me in Key West and Hurricane Matthew.

Tonight we ate ice cream sundaes on Duval Street, sitting on plastic chairs,

        Barb and Kelly and me, we three mayors of this little island town, road

        flooded with neon green t-shirt-wearing bridesmaids staggering in despair,

        and a staggered singing cast

        from open windowed trucks.

wading through a propensity for nostalgia: Jay and Brad sat

        in Con Leche sips, said hello to Motorcycle George and Brad heard

        the call *HOME.* Wide-eyed, he said, "I'd really like to live here." (2003)

Did you hear the news story about Mason Wells, who suffered
burns and shrapnel injuries in the Brussels terrorist attack after surviving the Boston Marathon and Paris
bombings?[100]

My phone, my albatross, turned on and found a new
envelope icon
text message waiting there from you: *I'm sorry. I was just overwhelmed.*
In the middle of the timeline:[101]

[WEST PALM BEACH]

Before I disembark.
According to Facebook, today is Wallace Stevens's
birthday. The Academy
of American Poets included this quote:

---

[100] See Walter De Maria "The Lightning Field," 1977.

[101] "If time is infinite, infinite / before and after, I wonder if the fish / ate my father's ashes. He once dynamited /
Flathead Lake, and now the two are even." from "Missoula," by [REDACTED}. Appeared in *Hanging Loose*, 81, 2002.

I was of three minds,

Like a tree

In which there are

three blackbirds.

Angela once likened Brad to him. I can see it now.

The meditation, the long walks out of Manhattan in a fugue state, the window photo

he sent with raindrops defined on polarized glass. Everything outside. Everything inside. Here in the parking lot of West Palm Beach, the train stopped with engineers

overlapping instructions over sleeper car

speakers, sun glares on automobile hoods. What good

are these Henry Flagler commemorations in the background, spires of stucco and sundrenched tile, when the pounding shine of light

can't caress polymer paints but strips it. Those fashion plate resorts we spy cross their legs and squat, either holding back urination or embarrassment.

What could be more beautiful than blushing? I can see this architecture bend.

Without oxygen, you suffocate. With oxygen, you rust.

I'm always the woman. Just different parts of her. Not always
her declaration. Not even always her drowning. Not
even always her tears and expression. Not all the dots.
Maybe just trapped behind Plexiglass and meaning different
things to different
people, but apart.

130

Francis Suspin spoke about pouring seventy-five-pound bags
of rocks and stones to scatter around a curving walk. The workmate he'd found
an iPhone photo of—a man laying down, ecstatic, in the open-armed joy
of completion—was named, get this, Ishmael.
Brad sent a postcard he'd bought on the drive back through
Pittsfield in Arrowhead, a shot of Melville's desk and the Greylock view;

white flakes and stones and rocks there in the distances,
in the yawning ground beneath us, in fingertips pressed insistently near glass, in unmistakable emerging.

131

Like everyone in the world, Brad feared pending meteors

as nearing. He wondered before those impacts what
each soon-to-be cratered head had thought in want. Chamber

Music heard as dots, notes placed along sheets, like
birds perched up on phone lines. Step back, it blends. You hear

elevator door gears engage—CLICK—in a shutter
sound for openings near torqued turns. Without these slivered

smiles to still ballerinas, though, and women crouched;
or the peering leer predating

Toulouse-Lautrec, Degas couldn't have filled a
stovepipe hat with the embers of his urging.

132

Ryan Grater stood back from the payphone. What happened?
Hours earlier, Brad had been kicked out of a
Manhattan bar he'd never even stepped
foot in. The destination for most road trips
used to be THE END, but Butch and Sundance heard
murmuring mouths set to growling, saying now, Get Out.
"She didn't like the state I was in,
and she didn't like the state I was in." Grater hung up
the receiving end. (1999)

Brad turned, his hand extended to say hello, and faced a famous
actor at a meeting three floors up the steps in Midtown.
He grinned
and said hello. (2010)

133

Stanza Three of *Trace* from September 30:

From wherever spring arrives
to heal the ground, from wherever searching rises
in a human being. The looking itself is a trace
of what we are looking for.

134

Dear Angela:

In this letter, there should be more cars. Back then, my father drove a red

MG. Question: How does one

respectively acknowledge a Dear John/

Dear Brad, preemptive break-up letter?

In my case, probably with more

picture-words. Forgive me. I knew you'd tell me I was creepier than Degas.

Translation: Thank you for your letter. It meant a lot.

Hold me at arm's length. Hold me at train
tracks length. My hands
are open for you to navigate. The irony now, beyond all this wanting,
is your desire to hold me at the length
of the East Coast and me,
somehow wanting to tell you everything.

After road trips, women are typically ready
to strangle me.

We'd have to avoid Charleston (a trap door)
and possibly Phoenix,
Arizona. Unfold and hold out your maps again.
I could make out
every word.

xo,
Degas

135

Brad's father played records in the morning; His favorite was
42nd Street. "That's the avenue I'm taking you to, 42nd Street." Brad'd be
rolling around on the pullout couch in that studio

apartment in Alameda, California.

He'd be blow-drying his hair. Brad'd be moaning in exhaustion.

He'd be singing into his brush. Those nights

they'd stay up late

and watch *Cheers*. Brad's father, newly sober with *Member's Only* jackets and a Mazda RX7, parked outside in the carport. Brad's father

as Sam Malone.[102]

---

[102] From Brad's South Lake Tahoe ski bum apartment last winter he watched every single episode, ever, of *Cheers.* The first season is among the best television stories ever made. The first episode is among the best pilots ever made. A telephone and an empty bar; a pretty intellectual woman poet and a sober alcoholic man. *Give Me A Ring Sometime* is the name of the episode. Give me a ring. The last time you texted, he explained "I have a new telephone on its way." You said, "I'm glad you're getting a new phone." What a funny thing for a phone phobic woman to say. Brad should have texted back, "I'm glad you're getting a new airplane." (Incidentally, in 12 Step slang, Telephonitis is a thing: When a drunk blacks out and starts making calls. Brad was blessed to get sober before cell phones. One winter he broke up with another Lisa in a blackout and didn't remember why. He asked Kyle, "Whatever happened to Lisa?" and Kyle kept saying, "You guys were awful." But he'd get drunk and sneak away to Grater's room and dial phone numbers like remembering a pin number for an ATM card. Brad finally got through). (Brad once thought the reason he had so much trouble with alcohol was that ATM's had been invented. He'd go out to MaryAnne's in Cleveland Circle with a folded up twenty in his acid washed jeans with no jacket on—because he couldn't afford to lose another—and cross the icy street all night, losing his money, one pin number memory at a time).

Sara, the weightlifter, spoke to Brad just before Sara, the Bareilles, started singing in his extra-large headphones. At his Key West gym, there's a singles scene of Florida lean and bulky getting closer at the Universal Machines. There's Brad, listening to a variety of soundtracks for the fiasco of his fitness, today "Manhattan" by Sara Bareilles. If you'd told Brad at age 22, Wu blaring in the bass tones of dilapidated rides—sound systems bending those orange defrost lines on the back window through the tilted Obscura of the rearview—he'd be listening to Sara Bareilles and loving it. Well.

He thought about New Hampshire Girl as a future ex-girlfriend; The Granite State as place and feeling too. What was it about Boston boys and New Hampshire girls? He'd dated Becky (sort of), Iris (sort of), and Alyce (with a y).

Heidi just started sending him naked photos on Facebook after he'd been six months in the gym. And now Sara of the muscular legs had him pondering different workout schedules. What would sex with a girl whose thighs made 70 days of skiing last season look like he'd grown a pair of toothpicks be like? What would it be like to plan abs and cardio, shoulders, bi's, back and chest on days Sara would be unlikely to be sickened by his Bareilles songs? The requirement of any altercation is escape routes.

[I'm starting New York with leaving this time. So what are your cathedrals?]

136

Despite your confession about telephone phobia, this collage somehow addressed to you

will be filled with telephones: Phone lines, phone poles, drawn lines, train tracks, highway lines, and maps.

After we finished texting tonight, I went on Instagram, a preview of the evening's

Chamber Music ensemble. You cannot hear in phone screenings; I'm watching

previews of evenings on my smartphone television screen

in Maryland. There's sound and bows gliding over lines. You're sitting down,

chin pointed now. I'm leaving on a train.[103]

Selina lived in Bel Air, Maryland, only a few miles

---

[103] Brad took a photo out the window of the train in Baltimore. A pair of conductors talk. A post is dark and black off-centered from the train parked in opposite direction. These men wear stark white shirts. He edited. He edited some more. He titled the image 'Ode To Kenneth Koch' and made a hashtag in reference to Monet's work in train stations (*The Saint-Lazare Station*, 1877, a 37 year old man homesick for the country). All that smoke. Incidentally, before Brad got sober (got is the wrong word) he took a photo class. In the dark room, shaky and still half drunk, he used a can opener on a film roll and slipped. When he opened the door, blood poured down his hand and shaky elbow. Blood leaked against the floor.

from where I just shot

a photo out the train window. I didn't have any idea where I was

for this "Meditation in Gray" but seemed to be caught

in the thought of you, looking

longingly out the train.[104]

I have this image of Jackson Pollock as a giant

throwing black strands of paint

across the United States in the shape

of interstate highways. Eisenhower hates

the Socialists but loves their Nazi efficiencies. He commandeers the Abstract Expressionists

to win the Cold War before it starts. There are always ways to break a treaty.

Take my father in cowboy boots and Paul Bunyan, combined into Jackson Pollock

and Richard Serra throwing molten lead: this is the start of men and women

throwing a set of nets over landscape. Take Herman Melville

[104] Brad's father worked as a train engineer on the Hungry Horse Dam. He dug some, and worked some, but mostly drove the train from underground. When Brad asked what he hauled, his dad replied "shit." He mostly stayed in charge of emptying latrines. True story: When Brad was younger, he wondered how his father had so many stories. Today he understands. (Did I ever tell you: Brad's Great Uncle was the Town Drunk in Hungry Horse, Montana?)

and *Moby Dick*, sprinkle

in Nathaniel Philbrick[105]—shower *Ahab's Wife*[106]—and the harpoon knives the waves keep slicing will sew until circles rise and form.

137

At the meeting, Brad thought: cathedrals.
Rothko at the Whitney, his new body healed
from nail holes he'd spurt stigmata with years
before; Lake McDonald and the reflections
of infinity, as my father has occupied
each dimension of sky and surface, stone.
My father had become the first fire, glacial melt,
and bone. Frank O'Hara in a letter, the parking lot
in Missoula. The first time I ever met you,
you wore long black boots and a scarf. In the dark
outside your Boston house, my eyes, like fingers

---

[105] Best commercial nonfiction prose artist since Irving Stone. See *Mayflower*. See *In The Heart of The Sea.*

[106] *Ahab's Wife: Or, The Star-Gazer,* a haunting book by Sena Jeter Naslund, combined with the Melville and the Greylock to sew a net to catch Brad in Greylock's shadow. He put white stones in his pockets and stood back. He put more and more in. An elevator waits. (Owen Chase, a survivor of Essex, Moby Dick's inspiration, hoarded food in his attic. Brad kept hoarding arrowheads and stones).

on the floor, searched around your mouth.

Brad told Angela in his mind: Curate Hopper's train tracks
next to Monet's lily garden and everything's explained.
Is this what higher learning is? A collage—one step,
and then another—a dance of flight starting with two
feet? Jasper Johns and his fingerprints are smeared everywhere
in here.

138

Some people think pilgrims stopped by the improbable beauty
of Plymouth Rock froze after those thousands of miles
of gray-green, the color of ice that's been crystalized so long
shattering's
forgotten—they believe gray granite stilled rudders
and rose Lazarus hopes inside; rose like cathedral
stones building upon themselves;
rose like cannonballs in stacks on the courthouse
lawn. But no, Eel River, the snake of blue right next
door to Brad's childhood home,
freshwater roping, rowing, into sea, carved the
sprawling words in cursive script through Butterflyweed, Little
Blue Stem, and Saltmeadow Hay: *Cathedral, Home, and Pray.*
No one would have stopped
for that famous and deplorable rock. A coastline filled
with whale's teeth

in open maw invitations, the symbols of stay away.

Snapping turtles the size of hubcaps, submerged and nibbled
cygnet legs;
lived beneath seagrass waving toward inlet eyes. He'd cast
and cast

and fall. Brad flailed in murk. Fresh water-filled pockets
and his shoes;
grasped and pulled his lungs. Brad learned
desperation before he ever learned how to swim. His
mother's back-of-matchbook resentments
demanded his father learn and teach him. "It's just
like riding a bike and a horse," those reflected river men might
say.

139

Rumi's trace points again in the direction
of an arrow. God is my Cupid.
In North Adams, that night, looking at you walk
Brad realized later
he'd been shot.

140

Brad's father always said:

[ ]

141

Brad felt less crazy about the missives, and the way

Williamstown reflected against the broad lawn, yawning, against the impatient and petulant sky, when he

remembered a meditation he'd written to himself (assembled in paper

hole punch outs) in early September

before he left Key West.

God is my manager.

God is my watch.

God is my investment banker.

God is my travel agent.

God is my night. God is my light.

God is my sky, and the bend

in God's own eye.

God is my hourglass

and my missing remote control.

God is my copilot's boss.

God is my curator and auctioneer.

God is my Cupid.

God's my grocery store.
God is nails behind the frame
and the holes made in the wall.

God is my auto mechanic.
God is my conductor, my train station.
God is the green dots on ancient Departure Signs.
God occupies the muck, green moss below fishing lines tangled before an undertow learns bodies wait for mangling.

And so it goes.

142

I had planned a system to count the dots. I had made a
printout of the painting
and brought a yellow highlighter pen so that I could count the
dots in a section
of the painting, write down the number of dots in this section,
then highlight
the section in my printout so that I wouldn't count the same
section twice.

I was planning to do this for the whole painting while at
MoMA, but I soon realized

that it would take much longer than I had expected, so I took
several close-up photographs
of the painting, went home, and continued counting the dots
there, using my photographs
as reference. This tactic proved much easier than trying to
count the dots at the museum

since I could sit down comfortably while counting, but it was
still incredibly
labor-intensive, and I gave up after two hours. I'm sure that I
could have arrived
at a pretty accurate estimate if I had been willing to invest
8-10 hours in this task,
but it seems to me that it would be impossible to settle
on a definitive final

dot count since the dots overlap in some parts of the painting
(i.e. the girl's lips).[107] I gave up counting after 1049 dots.

---

[107] From *The Drowning Girl Project*, a project Brad invented after leaving New York, after leaving everything, so he could have an excuse to revisit Angela in the water through a hundred-hundred eyes. He'd posted an ad on Craigslist and paid strangers fifty bucks a pop to look and look and look.

143

[DOT COUNTING SONNET]

Elevators elevate;
cathedrals rise;
mirrors reflect;
whaleboats capsize.

A River Runs
Through It;[108] tears[109] cleanse;
phones call; art prays;
photographs with bending lens
            pretend your friends
            won't end.

---

[108] Brad's father looked exactly like Robert Redford's surrogate son—Brad Pitt—in this tear-jerking masterpiece missive to Montana and alcohol and families and surrender. Kathy and Bennett Murgatroid lived right across the street from the church used during filming when Missoula became a town full of yellow leaves and collage. Brad himself fished in that same Blackfoot from the book/film. His Uncle Dave watched.

[109] The fact that tears (eye leaks) and tears (ripping) are spelled the same way is an example of language being the lover you cannot understand; an example of a page full of Ben Day dots saying, "Press your face and inhale."

Mirrors wait, and elevators open.
A tree needs water to grow. Closed mouth
don't get fed. Open your mouth to save
your life. Thousand-pound phone, feather light

drink. Drink drank drunk; sink sank sunk.
Phone lines, phone poles, harpoon strikes

144

Brad's father always said:
"You look like you've been shot at and missed
and shit at and hit."

145

Lisa Montague asks Brad via text if he ever heard of the
Buddha Horse.
Lisa Montague: Lovely, and Southern and smart and empty from over-swiping
on Bumble and Tinder after her divorce.

Brad called her Scarlett after Scarlett O'Hara.[110]

---

[110] Brad also called her "Frank O'Hara's niece" because he was his father's son and everybody deserves a river/tree of a family, a pedigree

She called him

Unicorn because he was a semi-smart painter still unmarried. They had coffee on this trip.

She meant the Buddha story:

There is a Taoist story of an old farmer who had worked his crops for many years.

One day his horse ran away. Upon hearing the news, his neighbors came to visit.

"Such bad luck," they said sympathetically.

"Maybe," the farmer replied. The next morning the horse returned, bringing three

other wild horses. "How wonderful," the neighbors exclaimed.

"Maybe," replied the old man. The following day, his son tried to ride one of the untamed horses, was thrown, and broke his leg. The neighbors again came to offer their sympathy on his misfortune. "Maybe," answered the farmer. The day after, military officials came to the village

---

of poetry and images to define them. How else would the world know the sound of ocean water without Turner and that mast? Across the vast distances of America, telephone poles raise their arms in protest; a series of paintings by Manet, remaking Goya's *The Third of May, 1808*. Angela told Brad in an inter-gallery whisper, "Manet." What is it about the decibels in museums that remind gilded frames of fingertips they haven't felt in years despite the curves and craving?

to draft young men into the army. Seeing that the son's leg was broken,

they passed him by.

The neighbors congratulated the farmer on how well things had turned out. "Maybe,"

said the farmer.[111]

146

There is the Lichtenstein imitation where we've been replacing

all his dots with crosses, still unfinished in the corner, and there is kissing you: Close-up

of a close-up of a painting of a comic book leaned-up against stark white studio

wall. The canvas plaster soaked-up with black and white and flesh tones

in X's, pores exposed from touch.

There is your yellow shirt swirled with reds and blues, flecks of black-white dots

wrinkled in spots; stretched in spots; wrinkled and

stretched flat against your skin,

my skin, my hands, our breaths, the painting, the painting leans. There is kissing you

---

[111] Directly lifted from http://www.katinkahesselink.net/tibet/zen.html

and there are the two of things: The two of us with brushes, taking liquid to push

up against the painting, against the wall, the two of us

painting.

I told you yesterday I don't dream much anymore, and then

last night there was

makeup everywhere. My nose, your nose, our cheeks, my blue shirt, bronze stars

turning us gold in light, turned us toward each other, toward the Lichtenstein imitation,

us intertwined with colors finding themselves, finding you, finding me, and phone calls

filled with empty space, words unsaid. There are spots unpainted. There are yellows,

still, to paint her hair with.

147

There's an infographic emoticon outside the men's room at

the MoMA, a black silhouette[112] with fat baby legs, fat baby head, fat baby arms. It reads:

BABY CHANGE. Another vote as girls—these *Drowning Girls*—pose against the Basquiat, more poem here than picture, a glass frame protects

---

[112] Variations on a theme by Kara Walker.

milk wash sticky gum sealing coloring pages and meandering. Brad laughed. His glasses

on, he laughed. They asked him, Can you move? He laughed. Baby change,

baby change, baby you need to change, he laughed.

In the bathroom, Brad takes a selfie, waits to see if Manet and

Degas sit in adjacent stalls. Which version of art history do you prefer? Alfred Barr as CIA, or Jasper Johns as

God? Look at all those fingertips and lips. New York steadies herself after discordant traffic streams—a tribute to

cathedrals—these misplaced

map-marked points; this field of Pop Art poppies.

Brad almost took a photo of a truck outside the entrance; a

garbage rig covered in graffiti signatures. What's more artistic: A Cadillac parked outside your rented house, the rooms a curse of vacant bookshelves,

or a truck idling

waiting at the red light, idling beside the MoMA?

Everything in the world can be a stand-in for an entrance; a photograph of your best

friend smiling next to Basquiat and tickling his ghost, or a memory of a porch light,

postcards left inside the breezeway, or those unanswered phone calls shaking tendons in the arm, unwrapped in electricity.

148

Watching Jeopardy with his mother, she thinks Brad

should tryout. But you're right,

brilliance comes in knowledge as well as system processing speed. Last week

Trebek said “Lichtenstein” as a category, and meant the country first. But in Double Jeopardy

Brad only went 3 for 5 on Roy. Keith Haring dresses

and accessorizes everyone here, and Frank O'Hara taught them the beauty of concrete. For me, NYC is *Desperately Seeking Susan*, dancing spins and swirls; Madonna[113] in Impermanent Cathedrals.

149

My dad blasting *42nd Street,* me listening to *New Found Glory*

redo “Crazy For You,”

the soundtrack skewed by time. I already told you about holding the red wire

when the phone rang, how tendons tensed and whined. I covered my closet walls

with comic book covers in High School, and covered

---

[113] Pick any Madonna. Give birth to a popstar seducing Basquiat.

my bathroom in *Art In America*

covers in Fort Point after college. Tell me, how did you prepare for your internal graffiti?

My books on the hotel room's coffee tables and knickknack coves; street art,

and flowers. Have you ever heard of Harry Geldzhaler[114] and what he brought on trips?

150

Hurricane updates: They just evacuated Guantanamo.

I used Guantanamo

for the setting of a novel once, *Art Official.* The book explored the Federal Government using a man named Arthur

Oswald Fischel to create an art world

resurgence during the War in Iraq and thereby boost the American economy.

In truth, the art world did boom during these lackluster

economic times. Best investment

you could have made at the start of that war was a Claude Monet. But when you told Brad you guarded the Guttenberg, he thought you meant the character in *Police*

Academy. Two lives causing ripples to rise in the soap

---

[114] See the film, *Who Gets to Call It Art?* from 2006. Harry hated hotel art, lugged invaluables in luggage.

suds of the sink. Two disciplines,

and commerce. Someone at The Cedar's sipping drinks.

There's a true precedent for this sort of thing.

Hemingway, the Ab Exers,

all sorts

got funds from the CIA. Hem was probably a spy.
The AbExers maybe didn't know. Alfred Barr,

the curator of MoMA got funds for Jasper Johns

and suns.[115]

When I think of Guantanamo, I think of Aaron Sorkin. I can handle the truth. He has

a MasterClass on the internet.[116] I have footnotes like footprints in the sand,

a man walking with peg leg.

---

[115] See *The Cultural Cold War: The CIA and the World of Arts and Letters* by Frances Stonor Saunders, The New Press, 2001.

[116] Brad took a one-night screenwriting class once. The instructor asked for their favorite character of all time from a movie. Brad said, "Brad Pitt in *True Romance*."

151[117]

The night after you apologized
Iris sent a picture text
(9:37 AM) of a book in focus
on her lap, her shoes and apartment distant,
blurred:

> "One has to commit a painting," said Degas,
> "the way one commits a crime." But you constructed
> boxes where things hurry away from their names.
>
> Slot machine of visions.
> condensation flask for conversations
> hotel of crickets and constellations.

---

[117] Brad considered using dots in random varying amounts as the numbering system for this collage. He also considered using numbers shuffled out of order as section headers (as with the poem "Counting" by [REDACTED] from Hanging Loose #79, 2001). Another thought was losing count and starting over, as someone would do when counting the Lichtenstein Ben Day dots this collage is constructed from. Or, having a single Ben Day dot on each side of each section header number. The space between, a near clichė thanks to the *Dave Matthews Band* song of the same name, always permanent and essential; the space between before Mr. and Mrs. Pac-Man meet in the middle and head up toward Heaven, gobbling bright spots along the way, impossible to traverse outside video game arcades.

Minimal, inherent fragments:
the opposite of History, creator of ruins,
out of your ruins, you have made creations.[118]

Brad replied after praying.

Who the #@!$ is that?
10:12 AM

Paz
10:36 AM

I'd been looking for the
perfect piece to send you
of this collection. I can mail
it to you when I'm done if
you want. It's hyper-meta
10:36 AM

I would like you to send me
the title of that poem at
the very least. I'm working

---

[118] The citation is on its way, two pages from now. Footnotes are an elevator. Push the button and wait.

on a collage and Degas
makes appearances. Also,
I just finished telling a guy
about the importance of
lens reflex photography
because of the warping of
lines. I didn't tell him about
the warping of Degas'
worldview and morality
as evidenced by the
constraints of a line type
he and Manet claimed they
stole from Velasquez (read:
appropriated) at the same
moment in the Louvre. I
laughed on the beach,
tilted my chin toward the
deformity of coast, some
so he couldn't see me
and mistake my smile
for superiority, and some
because the tiny pebbles
in the middle smooth
between white sand (read:
stolen from Ohio) and

ocean were rendered in an unnatural undulation of outlines Degas would have had to use obscura for. We see the world upside down to figure it cleanly.[119]
10:43 AM

! How fortuitous!
10:44 AM

Get some boots or high heels or something. Those slippers aint got catwalk written all over them, unless you bought a leash for your feline.
10:45 AM

When speaking of the

---

[119] This is when Brad knew the collage was almost over. I did too. I had started writing texts in preparation for inclusion. The experiment had been polluted by the experimenter. Still, I prayed every day, "God, I thank you for all these connections. Please keep revealing yourself to me." A few days before, a man named Craig hugged Brad at the start of a meeting and Brad almost wept.

Spanish poets, please
make the first exclamation
upside down.
10:45 AM

@Hahahah they're not
slippers, they're Keds!
10:46 AM

What's the poem title,
"Platform Keds and Kitten
Walks?"
10:52 AM

<Subject: NoSubject>
(Here reader, is where you imagine
a black and white paperback
cover. Bottom left, emerging,
arm folded on suit, as if in allegiance
to a political party, or about to rip
his throat and heart out as elegantly
as possible, so as not to scuff
the white shirt cuffs, a photo of a poet.
Above: SELECTED POEMS.
And below: OCTAVIO PAZ)

10:53 AM

The poem title; the poem
(upside down exclamation)
10:54 AM

<Subject: NoSubject>
“Objects & Apparitions”
for Joseph Cornell
10:55 AM

152

What about those hawks
I thought
when I saw the egret stroll
behind the grocery store today.

My father’s ashes in Flathead Lake, scatter.

153

These dots, these stand-ins for consumers unthinkingly
standing at attention for commands—the
advertised—are confined by dark lines throughout,

sequestering. Confinement heightened by
composition strategies: women pressed to edges, military
men caught beneath attack fighter canopies, lovers
entangled and tied in arms, narrators tortured by encroaching
word weight in mushroom-cloud thought balloons;
dialogue boxes pressing down at flesh.

Lichtenstein applied dots with a stencil and a toothbrush, a
process akin to Chinese children toiling in iPad
assembly lines rather than romantic dances
round and round taught canvas
made famous by AbExers.

154

Remember, I told you about Mickey, the murderer
turned spiritual advisor saying, "Come Home."

Today after I meditated, I looked down at the pillow
from my rented apartment furnishings setting
on the floor. HOME[120] it said, embroidered
and unmistakable in needlepoint dots.

---

[120] It didn't *say* this in real life. It *read.* But for the purposes of this dot collage, the pillow spoke.

155

There are a dizzying 2 trillion galaxies in the universe,
up to 20 times more
than previously thought, astronomers
reported on Thursday.[121]

The Orionids meteor shower starts tonight, the first major
since the Perseids; the former brought in Mark Twain with Comet Halley before his orbiting
prophecy announced boomerang returns would take him away. Lichtenstein's sky,
still and permanent, revised with these irrational fire strikes from somewhere on the other side, from Bill de Kooning and his eyes revising lines at a cocktail
party in a high rise. When he left Ashville, he saw Fitzgerald's wife on fire.

When he saw the WOMAN pictures, he set them near the trash outside. What makes
a person go back inside three times to check if the coffee pot's unplugged?
What's the difference between substantial bouts of

---

[121] *The Guardian,* Thursday 13 October 2016 14.55 EDT. (Earth, and all our parallel multiverses as well; look over there beside you. There's another you in all those infinities of adjacent dots).

OCD and a bad memory?

Angela said: If we spent more time together, you'd have to revise your thoughts

of me. Brad built Kleenex rafts on top of tear-

streamed seas. De Kooning

hanged those paintings in effigy and looked back past the shed where Arshile Gorky

swung. Without retouching all these dots and eyes, how can anything get redone? When we get back to land, Brad thought, I promise to revise our shore.

I heard you cry. I understand. Behind the crowds, the dark line widened

gasps from the elevator doors.

156

How to prepare for a hurricane: The people next door place Jesus crosses

on their windows in masking tape. They cross their hearts and hope to crucify, revise. Seeing you

in The Berkshires nudged me into another nothing,

another something. What is it like to share your bedroom secrets, to secrete

lipstick stains and sweat, eye-watering shakes, and finger clutches with a person

you desire and admire? An arrow bolted me off path

and knocked me now
next door. Meanwhile, can you tell Melville's home is
named Arrowhead?

I know you're watching the news. It's so easy to be worried.
It's so easy
to confuse anxiety with desire. In The Berkshires,
some of us realized
admiration and longing can coexist. It's why I'm not gnashing
teeth. Despite the difficulty communicating when two
artists find themselves out of phones and out of airplanes—
scattered haphazardly in toothbrush bristle
spots—I'm guessing you watch the news and worry.

What else is the news for? Closed Captions dislodging
meanings; typos tuned
to sounds, as inconsistent as a man with a Boston
accent saying, "Okay Google" with more and more
desperation. "Siri, fucking understand me, please."
Please. Emotional OCD is diagnosed as bad memories
I just keep coming back to.

157

What was your experience like with Drowning Girl?

I had seen reproductions of the painting, but I'd never seen it in person so its size impressed me. Other than that, I knew the painting very well since I used to have printouts of his painting glued to my high school agenda. I love the painting as much as I did back then. It also made me think of the artist Nicolas Moufarrege, who appropriated *Drowning Girl* in his 1984 embroidery *Drowning Rug*, made while he was dying of AIDS.

Have you ever had the feeling of drowning? When and in what situation did this occur?

Yes. About ten years ago, I was deeply depressed, and I felt like I had no control over my feelings and might go insane or die (though not by suicide).

Have you ever felt like the girl in the painting? Have you ever felt like Brad? Explain.

As mentioned above, I've had the feeling of drowning (metaphorically), but I've never felt like I would rather give up hope than ask for help. To me, that's a cowardly reaction. Although the painting itself is beautiful (conceptually and in terms of composition and execution), I have no sympathy for the drowning girl. She strikes me as childish, melodramatic, and self-centered. As far as I can tell, Brad is either a figment of the girl's imagination or someone onto which she is projecting feelings and

intentions. Brad is like Jareth the Goblin King, David Bowie's
character in the movie *Labyrinth*. Brad is probably
painting in his studio or having cocktails with the yellow-haired girl while this one is sinking.[122]

158

On the surface of the water, the storm is forming. If those dots create a colander

when you look through a Lichtenstein, which parts of you go through,

and which parts stay behind? If you're looking at a Lichtenstein as a Monet

waterlily painting, which parts of you reflect back and which parts

reside beneath or are obscured like roots and bottoms? God is moving

like de Kooning is God's finger in your living room, swirling in his cocktail glass,

before revising a painting you've shelled out half a fortune for and to.

Saul Bellow: "We are funny creatures. We don't see stars as they are, so why

do we love them? They are not small gold objects but

---

[122] From Claudia Eve Beauchesne's response to *The Drowning Girl Project*, October 15, 2016.

endless fire."[123]

Brad's father always said:

"In this house, we follow the Golden Rule: The man with the gold

makes the rules."

159

Younger girls, this one named Alyce, gobbled up Brad's mouth once. He was

such a narcissist he thought she exclusively used purple heart emojis for him

to see [a field of faces]. He looked deeper into the water and let his eyes adjust to these

reflections. He saw the moon quiver. He saw lily pads. He saw the heart.

He saw the heart disappear.

Monet controlled three eternities in those late lilies without horizon. Surface, submerged,

and sky; past and present, future. Francis Suspin gave a lecture on these sunsets

reflecting skies on fire. Look through the forms carved

---

[123] *Henderson the Rain King*, Penguin Classics Edition, 2012 (first published in 1959), page 276.

from the flat glass dimension and find the

pieta; Jesus twisting in negative space.

Alyce and Brad broke up, and there was a selfie convention at *Jeff Koons: A Retrospective,*

a show Brad caught down at The Whitney. Jeff Koons as prophet, predicting museum

visitors finding themselves in gazing balls and glossy aluminum balloons. Find yourself

in those Lichtenstein dots, take a picture in the reflection on the glass. Love is give

and take. People didn't even look anymore without a translator; they looked at Rothko

through smartphone screens. Angela and Brad talked at the Clark. How can a painting be your favorite when dulled by reproduction? I am in my screen digging.

Alyce didn't come. He sent a photo of the aluminum *Hanging Purple Heart.*[124]

---

[124] See "New York Man Charged After Vandalizing Jeff Koons Show" in *Observer* by Nicole Vranjican, 10/20/14:

"A local man has been charged with criminal nuisance after spray-painting an interior wall of the Whitney Museum this past Saturday. The incident occurred when a rouge museum-goer graffitied large black letters on a wall near Jeff Koons' *Hanging Purple Heart*... ...leaving behind the word 'PPRRiceless' reflected in the nearby piece of art." "He misspelled the Posse's intended message 'PPPriceless' as 'PPRRiceless'" [graffiti in reflection; art criticism as typos, Alyce wrote obscured words on the reflecting side of Brad's Monkey Moon heart (see the story of the Monkey and the Moon, I'm running out of space]. On October 4 Alyce liked Brad's video on Instagram. When he

[LOVE IS GIVE AND TAKE][125]

The tugboat's tugging, taking ships out into ocean. White spots on waves

remind your cousin's family that mercy lay burning above the lake.

My father's ashes, sinking into water— sifting sand and crushed up bone, resistant

---

looked, the heart was gone. She may have hit HEART by mistake, making the video play or stop. His caption read "Playing Taylor Swift Backwards." It was a video he took when he left New York on September 17, the day after the Chelsea bomb. He'd been thinking about the Taylor Swift song "Welcome to New York," which seemed readymade for the program *Girls. Girls*, a program Brad shouldn't like. Taylor Swift, a singer Brad shouldn't like. Once, Alyce and Brad compared Taylor Swift notes. "I love that album," he said. "Never Go Out of Style." He wrote on his gratitude list that night, "I am grateful I didn't go crazy when I saw Alyce like that video." Three weeks later, he saw she had a new grey kitten. The story of America is finding things no one ever lost.

Other people's New York Memories: The story about Andre Breton and Mondrian, all those World War refugees. Breton wants to paint the entire city different colors—the roads, the buildings, the stop signs. Brad painted a painting with oil sticks called "Andre and the Butterfly." Skyscrapers shake and smear. Arhsile Gorky is everywhere: it's a story from the Spender biography in 2001. Breton sees the butterfly and turns Manhattan into a maze just trying to capture it.

[125] From the book *OxyContin for Breakfast* by Kurt Cole Eidsvig. Main Street Rag, 2023.

in the heat it faced, now combining into waves. We watched gray sky forever,

until all it did was take.

I'm giving you once last chance, your last eight-page apology letter might state.

I am taking it from the shoebox, from the pair of shoes you gave me in the shoe store

in Montana. I am giving it to the flames.

Take your sister, for instance, she's not married, yet. No one gives her a chance

to speak her mind. Blonde, empty hair taking its time to become her neck, her

shoulders— her waist and then her legs. Take in two more notches on that belt.

Take yourself up sharply. Take my name, my heart. Take my breath

so far away from here I won't remember how to speak. Take a chance. Take a dive.

Take and take and take.

Give yourself a break for once. Give this thing a chance. Give it one more day.

Give your mother a call, would you? You know how she gets worried. Give

me that. Give your daughter away. Give the gift that keeps on giving.

Take another look at that art print: Two black labs wearing two red, black lab dog collars,

each holding an end of leash in their mouth, or an extra-thick piece of spaghetti.

It reads: *Love is give and take.*

Take a look at yourself, for a minute, in the sheen from the reflected glass

of the frame. Give your hair a toss, and then just look again. Stare through

everything you see, and take it in. Love is give and take.

Did I mention my father's ashes yet? Take life and death, water and fire—

ocean, sky—bone, sand, flesh, and blood and mix

them in one moment. Take it with you

when you leave.

Give it away to the landscape, and give it all a chance to merge into the meaning

of everything. Take it away in a porcelain urn.

Burn it into

lake waves. Take your time in calling me back.

We are all forgetting something.[126]

---

[126] See *A Valentine's Ritual For One: Love in Many Acts,"* by

161

So, what do we do when the hurricane turns? What do we do

when the hurricane turns away? A thousand-thousand monkeys multiplying in a thousand-thousand moons, Brad never found himself

staring at the luscious ass of a woman he admired. In those empty spaces between nucleus and electrons—all of us made of more nothings than something—

is where those alternate dimensions lay, the multiverse as expounding worlds the physicists and quantum mechanics all tell us are there. They are next to us,

right here. Right there. That's where.

Stanza Four from *A Trace* by Rumi on September 30:

"But we have been more like the man

who sat on his donkey and asked the donkey

where to go."

Time is an hourglass filled with albatross necks.

And when I ask "why." I don't want an answer. I'm looking

for something I want to fix or argue with.

Vanessa Vartabedian, featuring this poem by the author. There are clips on YouTube. In the future, everybody gets a minute and 42 seconds of fame.

Brad thought about calling himself. Sighed. Decided

he'd rather die.

162

[Anselm Kiefer's *The Women of the Revolution*, 1992/2013. Seen at MASS MoCA]

Is there someone underneath that bed? That leaf, that single leaf. There are too many

names to be remembered. Is that the falling of a meteorite? How many catastrophes before you close your eyes? Is there a leak? There's a paint palette over there. Our bodies

leave indents. Our bodies, celestial bodies, leave rust. Our bodies are old pennies.

What are you walking away from? Our bodies leave.

How long before there's no more room underground for graves? I have gotten sleepy

since we work in shifts here (a security guard sighs). Even the tourists are overwhelmed.

163

Me? Brad thought. I was so confused with piece of mind and

peace of mind

when I was new, that I made a collage of jigsaw shapes glued down and organized

in a peace sign. Above, it reads, *PIECES.*

164

The difference between ellipsis and eclipses

is how dark you think

the rest will be and how long that darkness lasts.

The problem with life, and with text message exchanges, is you never know

when they'll end. If Lichtenstein's a colander, which parts of you

pass through, and how big is the wad of spaghetti-guts[127] your immersion

leaves behind? In the collage, the train is parked in Washington, DC. In my heart, I'm out in Western Mass. In the window's reflection, the world

is a treadmill, or an elliptical trainer, rather. I'm arriving at the train.

I'm arriving at the museum. I'm arriving at the end.

---

[127] See the entire oeuvre of James Rosenquist as logical Lichtenstein inheritor for an explanation of spaghetti.

From *Buffalo Tom*'s "Wiser:"[128]

Drive back
Drive back
        Drive back
Drive back

165

ALISTER LUSTRE
A onehundredpagepoem???
Holy moly! What's it about?
3:46PM

BRAD
It's a long meditation
that started as all
about New York, then
all about 37 minutes
at the Museum of
Modern Art, then just
about this woman,
this girl, and
everything. And now

---

[128] From the album *Smitten,* 1998.

it's all about Roy
Lichtenstein's
'Drowning Girl'
painting, which are
many different
arrangements of lines
recast and pressed
as Arabic alphabet
letters, telling you the
exact same thing.
3:53PM

ALISTER
Oh shit! That sounds
super intense and
cool. I'd love to see
the whole thing
pasted on the side of
a building in NYC!
3:54PM

166

Brad had a dream this morning during meditation
his chest had a skeet shoot catapult inside. My chest
(his chest) took launching hearts out seriously.

The point of life

was to throw your heart out far, let it float, let it rise like the gods; shimmer like Monet's cathedrals in the sun.

My mind (his mind) held the aiming rifle. If I (if he) lets it get

past my eyes, I blast it out of the sky.

This may have been influenced by Instagram artist

Emilio Garcia.[129] His art includes colored hearts made to look like hand grenades. HEART. HEART. HEART.

And BRAIN.

167

[Anselm Kiefer's *The Women of the Revolution*, 1992/2013. Seen at MASS MoCA]

[Part 2: Angela's still elsewhere; Angela's still here. I don't care; I'd rather sink]

Every life is a topographical nap. We sleep and leave indents behind. On every map

the net of lines casts from buried palettes. This is after the dinner party by Judy Chicago, as every arrangement has

---

[129] For more on Emilio Garcia and his work check his Instagram account @emiliogarcia.art

been before and after. Your name's a city cutting

things in half. Which lake used to be here before it dried? Up, look up, because

that's the direction things will dry in.

Sediment, sentiment, spectacles. See: Spectacles. No one plans a spectacle, and which

do we look at, and which do we look through? Look up. Look it up. Look it up and down in sullen trajectories and wonder at gravity's mechanics kicking in (kick-off,

kick in, dry off, pick up) sullen at the launchings of items lost into night. Light

casts, ideas swirl, tables turn; bet on it, see it through. Which version of mis-

remembered are you?

Suellen in Key West posts pictures of the things she collects in

seaglass green.

Bricks; foundation bricks. Flirtatious flotation bricks. What's above these beds? Everything suggests a landing: leaf, meteor, deposits, dents, names,

space, reflections, water, leaks, news, nets creeping out, another leaf, cookie crumbs, Schnabel plates, words, names, and a history of language. Van Gogh

remnants, numbers. Of course, you see the footprints. Shark fin, shark find,

shark fun. Ominous shark fin on grey sea coming after. Come after, come forward, come to.

Each bed is a container of the rotten ocean, a fascist more powerful than anything gravity

might fight as they try and sprout. In the other room are paintings of poems about

the sea, lead pressing seeds of waves as the bloom to orange-gray doom, lashed around mast

waists, the leeward slip toward mausoleum ships. Forget what's below, I tell you;

forget what waits below. [Look up at the baptismal. Look up at the porchlight]

In the bathroom mirror, in the mornings, Brad saw a rash grow across his cheeks and forehead

too. Red bumpy dots covered his skin increasingly with each glance. He was a man turning into a painting he'd appropriated from a medicine cabinet's blank face. Open the cabinet and see bottles of pills stacked and filled inside. Open the cabinet and watch the world

bend in your mind. Brad titled his life now: *Self-Portrait as a Lichtenstein.*

168

My first memory that surfaces is a kitchen sink in

Kingston, Mass; my father's first apartment after the divorce. Without a bathtub

I was so afraid of all that water shooting from a spigot

in the showered sky above. I know you don't like to take

showers, he said, my face peering around the bathroom door at the empty spot. He brought me to the kitchen, lifted me up above the long brown counter. It was, by far,

the biggest silver sink my three-year-old eyes had ever seen. Sit your ass down in that, he said, and ran the water warm, warm, warm, filled it with bubble bath. I love you so much, my son, he said,

and sprayed me with the black plastic gun all down my back, wiggling against the surfaces; slick skin and sliver bin, knees bent and fit inside

squared water, soap floating at the surface.[130]

Brad's father always said:

"I love you so much, my son, my son.

Do you know that?"

169

I knew your preemptive breakup had precipitated a premeditated heartbreak the night before the storm when Brad kept listening to *Buffalo Tom.*

I'm in this bar with you, but my mind must be back in San Francisco.

Highways. My head is loose at last. Radio's on full blast, and I'm rolling

---

[130] First printed in *Sourland Mountain Review*, 2016 by [REDACTED]

in a midnight Chevrolet.

I'm caught dead in the night / stars and firelights / the sky a jewel / I believe I'm back

in Boston.

And you're all across the moon / and you're all across the moon / and I'm lying

across the tracks / and you're on a train ride back. And you're all across the moon,

and you're all across the moon, and you're all across the moon.

Did I mention the aftermath of Matthew is on its way?

170

Walt Williams gets bridges and rest stops, the epigraph above a

beauty store

in Greenwich Village. They named the angels after you.

171

When Brad first did the Serenity Prayer as a suggestion to stay sober, he didn't know what serenity meant. He mistook the word for boredom. The Celebrity Prayer

came when he was at a meeting in NYC and a guy sat next to him, a few minutes late.

Brad turned and shook his hand before he realized he

was one of our favorite actors.

My friend Bryan in Lake Tahoe got paranoid when he started
shooting meth. He thought people in meetings were
videotaping his shares. A couple picked up a Red Bull
can he'd tossed down on the ground, said "Can we
collect this?" and he believed it meant they were fingerprinting
him rather than being passive-aggressive about littering.
He said to Brad on three-thousand-mile-long phones, "I have
something really crazy to tell you: I saw a famous actor
at a meeting in Reno, Nevada. Everyone was looking at him.
Crazy right, that I thought the whole meeting
was in on it, and out to get me?"

Brad said, "That actor is sober, loves to gamble, and goes to
meetings. That's the least crazy thing
you've said all day."

[I'm crazy for you. I'm crazy for you, baby]

A few months later, Brad's voicemail dotted calls from Tahoe.
Bryan walked in the woods and hung himself. The right
word is hanged. He walked in the woods
and hanged.

172

The death certificate said "Victim of Passive Aggressive Environmentalists."

In present[131] tense, this train just arrived in Sebring, Florida, alive. The rain has started spitting Morse Code dashes and dots against cabin windows. Closed Captioning

comes in clear, citing every explanation from the sky. Look up. Look up

the meaning. Look up at meaninglessness. And cry.

173

[ENTANGLEMENT TEAM FREES FEMALE HUMPBACK]

The Center for Coastal Studies in Provincetown freed a humpback whale

from an entanglement in fishing gear Wednesday

---

[131] Overheard at a meeting: The reason they call it the present is because it's a gift. If you are thinking about the past, you get depressed; think about the future, you get anxious. Yesterday is gone, history is a mystery. The future isn't here yet. Every day's a holiday when you're not drinking the first drink of alcohol. Every morning is Christmas because I'm unwrapping the gift of the present; the gift of my sobriety. Every night is Thanksgiving because I get down on my knees and thank my Higher Power for the gift. When I was drinking it was the opposite. Every day was the same. Every day as *Groundhog Day*, only getting worse and worse.

(10/19/16) off Cape Cod.

The whale, a mature female named Storm, was accompanied by her calf.

This is the second time this year Storm was disentangled, and the 20th

marine animal disentangled by CCS's Animal Entanglement Response team

this year.[132]

As Brad's father used to say:

"I'll tell you; I felt lower than whale shit."

174

WED 9:57PM

How do I remind you of Lichtenstein and vice versa?

THU 7:53AM

Because you're in love with him. Maybe more than Monet. Or, how to say it,

I bet the loves feel distinct. You're intertwined with him in my mind. Not Monet

though, because Monet reminds me of Paris and my mirror (his Poppy Fields sit at its foot). In any case, now

---

[132] *Cape Cod Times*, October 20, 2016 at 8:38 PM. Earth; this universe. Written by Ethan Genter.

you're writing a love song to him![133]

175

If love is what holds this world together,

as Roger Round said in his share

about looking at the face (i.e. the *Face of God*, the curve

of Earth at 50,000 feet) then is God just gravity?

God is holding us together. If so,

I'd rather sink.

Water, water everywhere,

and not a drop to drink.

Look at the branch.

Move over now and look at the branch's ghost. A circle where an arm used to be. The cycle of abandonment is marked in past dimensions,

breadcrumbs—perfect and round and regular—depending on your glance. Brad stood

for a while and stared at the Sargent; at Degas. He staggered breaths in and out

of chest while taking in the Kiefer. Brad stood in the

river.

---

[133] From Facebook messages with Iris.

176

"Usually, however, other people are involved. Therefore, we are not to be the hasty and foolish martyr who would needlessly sacrifice others to save himself from the alcoholic pit…

…He had commenced our way of
life, had secured a position and was getting his head above water."[134]

177

Roy had a career of paintings splitting atoms.

Light is a particle. Light is a stream.

Alcohol is a stimulant. Alcohol is a depressant.

Brad stood in the river. His father always said, "Women are like buses."

178

Without Matisse's *Red Studio,* Arshile Gorky never lives;

---

[134] *Alcoholics Anonymous,* Fourth Edition. New York, 1939, 1955, 1976, and 2001.

Rothko can't find the brushes,

and there are no brushstroke measures in A History of the Universe. Look at that clock,

the Grandfather Clock. Grandfather, the world is tectonic plates in red. The world is verging

on an earthquake. Action painting copies of antiquity, with smartphone touch screen   presses. They met. Make finger pads balled feet and meet this abstraction of the world.

I'm dancing. I'm dancing. My true art is a dance step on a smartphone. I'm looking

for something else in there.

179

Matthew made other Key West plans.[135]

Brad checked on his friend Laura in Daytona Beach.

LAURA

It's good. Wild out there

but safe in here

---

[135] Overheard at the Verizon store: "Matthew isn't coming. He left." "Oh yeah. Well, you left Key West too. What did you do? You came back."

BRAD

Sounds like the opposite of

your body and your brain!

Xoxo[136]

In all of this, our eyes are shards, our eyes

become irreparable,

our eyes are surely broken.[137]

180

Take a map. Take Matisse in a fishbowl. Take the fish. Take the birds. Take the cage. Brad once made a collage about Matisse neglecting everything he ever painted. He'd already consumed every nutrient those fruits and fish and women had to offer. Brad once followed Matisse's dietary advice, rowing daily and eating hardboiled eggs for lunch. His was on a lake. Brad's was in a live/work studio loft in Fort Point, looking out at the back of Southie. We can be so close to things and so far

---

[136] Before *Gossip Girl,* Brad signed missives XO. At first it was a lark. Brad, sending hugs and kisses. Then he did a whole series of artworks with them, XOXOXO and an installation. Bridger Murphy, Bennett Murgatroid. David Palmer said he liked the pieces, they reminded him of branding. Angela came to the show. X marks the spot on a map, O circles it. X and O as every letter, etc. Brad's cousins Constance and Reef asked if he was doing it because of his grandmother. Helen loved X and O.

[137] From "This Guernica," *Big Red & Shiny*, March 2, 2002.

away.

Be like Gauguin: Take Syphilis and give it to the locals. The gift that keeps on giving.[138]

Brad got a phone call from a sober alkie at the museum.

The kid has herpes.

There's nothing so bad a drink can't make worse.

---

[138] It just occurred to me that my love for Butcher Billy, the Pop Artist extraordinaire, isn't just because his craft is great (it is) but because he conflates rock stars and musicians with comic book heroes. This is something I've been doing for years. Only, in my poem "You're Probably in Japan By Now," I wrote "Just yesterday I realized I'd turned Mark Rothko into a character for my poems, / and how interesting paint and sound are compared to abstraction./

What a terrible tragedy to turn light— breaking to black fog— settling against/ a wall— or creating a wall— into a caricature or a person even. Love. /I do this to all things I love, which should be flattering, but is not—/ and now I have a strained relationship with *Untitled* from 1958." Back then I thought I was turning Rothko, Matisse, Gauguin. et al, into characters for poems. But I was actually turning them into comic book heroes and villains, their attributes notched up or down on the contrast scale. Lisa Montague sent me the often-reposted parable about the two dogs fighting inside ourselves the other day. One is good and love. One is pain and fear. Which one wins? The one we feed. Inside myself, myself a metaphor for adolescent and teenage walk in bedroom closets, myself a metaphor for artist live/work studio bathrooms, myself a metaphor for specific and far-ranging geography and books and music, there is a two dog fight in medias res. Only instead of dogs, it's the world's superheroes of art history. Many of them wear masks and emerge from phone booths clad in tights.

181

What could be more coincidental than all this talk of birds

and trees? Chuckie Klimt, a thousand miles away,

musing on the meant reminders of mustard seeds in sermons, he keeps whispering against the shore waves captured in picture-perfect window

squares without the glare, "But what, but what, but what does it mean?"

Tell me something: Is there any question Wallace Stevens

rode these tracks

to paradise when he cast aside the skyline for southernmost departures? There is a line; follow it. Follow something else.[139] Those blackbirds

in the trees often look simultaneous in their attention. Brad told Henry Zone recently, The problem with losing your

brakes in life is you can get along just fine without them for some amount of time.

When Brad thinks of landlocked hotel nightmares Florida creates, he thinks

of Michael Davis pounding automobile hoods into

---

[139] See *White Numbers,* by [REDACTED] originally published in *The Masthead*, Volume 1, Issue 3, Summer 2006.

novellas from sprawl.

He thinks of Michael Davis as the sun.

How long, Brad wondered, before I forgive myself for forgetting Pollock's feet?

182

Wordy, without arrival, longing, and imparting departures,

Wallace Stevens as airport lounge reminders of the places you could be. But Little Hem, and my father, this fishing on banks of rivers. I see Hemingway too, spare

and hard and mean at times. He hit everything he loved to make sure it could survive. After two plane crashes, he died from double-barreled sips. A gun,

a gun, a gun, I said, the double shot of cocktail he savored on his lips.

My biographers might describe my style as neither Hemingway nor Stevens, if there are biographers to rouse,

but more like the fistfight both of them had in a bar in Key West's Old Town.

He was aiming to create the child of John Donne

and Elmore Leonard

and missed.

There's a sky filled with quarters in case

you ever find a payphone.

183

Brad got an email back from Suspin confirming a mailing address. He decided

to send the Melville postcard view of Mount Greylock. His grandmother's whale was perched on church steeple in Plymouth, Massachusetts, too, the site

of the first 12 Step meeting Brad's father ever stuck to. The Eel River Group, named, of course, for fresh water. All of us are cast javelins and harpoons into black

wells of the past.

184

Porcupine quills, stereo speakers, heat vent holes

in the top of my cable box.

Metal park, or bus stop, benches; lots of shocked faces. Nowhere Man's scene

in *Yellow Submarine* "Sea of Holes/Green." Now that I look again, it appears

like a bunch of x's and arrows. The older monk picked up the woman, carried her across the river, placed her gently on the other side, and carried on his journey.[140]

---

[140] From Kindspring.org, *Two Monks and a Woman - a Zen Lesson* --

In this poem, there's a character who tattoos names
of towns against his skin. Instead of adjusting font
sizes for population growth, he increases their lines
based on the amount of things he left behind there.

In Marshfield, Massachusetts, a whole room stores
computers and disregarded furniture. In Key West
there are some books and music, a romance with
a jet ski instructor. In Chicago, there's tears and pride.

The biggest word written across his chest, by far,
is your name. Access roads like veins spread out
from careful letters and stretch along to freckles
of surrounding towns. Light fingernail tip touches
consider relationships between shapes and sounds
and flesh in the exhausted haze of just before
and after. After and before.[141]

Finally, the younger monk couldn't contain himself

any longer,

blurting out, "We're not permitted a woman, how
could you then carry that woman?"

The older monk replied, "I set her down on the other side

of the river, why are you still carrying her?"[142]

---

by Ahlhalau, posted Jun 20, 2014.

[141] Originally published as part of *Big Red & Shiny*, Volume 2, Number 11, August 13, 2013, "23 Exit Signs."

[142] Also adapted from Note 137.

You look at Lichtenstein and you think of me;
I look at Lichtenstein
and think of everyone in the world.

185

Found a photo in my smartphone of a long orange extension
cord undulating across the tiles in my old rented apartment in Key West.

I titled the post on Instagram "Variations on a Theme
by Brice Marden." This happens to me on the time machine and elevator of life (look down at the sand). I see
artists' work after I complete a painting and realize I copied it without knowing they existed.
Examples: Jeff Koons and Superman at the ICA in 2007; Jackson Pollock and line drawings; Baldessari and
goldfish. Also, I see artist's work everywhere, like Brice Marden extension cords: Barnett Newman in the light space between two curtains in my loft; Kenneth Noland
through a window in a church's meeting room; the fire escape stairs. Alex Katz and Maine countrysides; Spencer Finch
and sunsets.

All of us do this, which is why Pop Art is so important. We
mine memory for anchors to what the world should be.

Norman Rockwell Thanksgivings,

Michelangelo, with God's finger stretching, stretched out, just about there;

an extension cord is a metaphor for everything.

186

At that coffee shop in Boston, Brad spoke to his mentor Suspin

about Lichtenstein's *Brush Stroke Group,* the artist's sculpture standing sentry at the harbor in Boston, Mass. "Have you read *The Art of Fielding*?" Brad asked. "At fictional

Westish College, on the shores of Lake Michigan, a Herman Melville statue cast looms tall, resists the wind." In Roy's case, the piece speared out toward ocean's

whitecaps, a paint stroke bent and frozen, tethered to base with rope line knotted in cleat's clear eye stare, attached to bold and sure aluminum harpoon.

187

Hardest Brad ever cried came on Flathead Lake while talking to his father. He went back three years after, saw the dot gather and approach, become a seagull, and thought, "I don't want to leave without you, Dad."

He painted a hundred paintings that year titled *We All Come Back as Birds* and the near-anorexic model Malaney lay on his bed and said, "Look," after he finished praying on his knees.

A hawk gripped metal fire escape, a hawk whose feathers shook.

He saw the nail in his cousin's shoe. The hole began to bleed.

188

Picking up his mail without more Angela scribbled notes,

Brad broke out the phone and congratulated Dolly on her Yankee Candle modeling. "Cover girl look," he said and resisted asking about girls and drowning. "Do you

prescribe scents for people's ills now?" they laughed. He flipped and found *Beachwalk*, and *Blue Summer Sky* and *Catching Rays* instead of "Roys."

Golden Sands and *Home Sweet Home.*[143] "You're fame," he said. But no votive burned as bright and clear as ambergris. No flame, no fire, alone.

189

Did you see the image of the woman hip-deep in water,

clutching the side of a building in Haiti,

after Matthew came storming through?

---

[143] Each one an actual candle product from The Yankee Candle.

190

Devi; we haven't texted in a while. Maybe since she told me Bryan hanged.

She's working at PR

for a horrible South Lake magician.

Brad: Are you the girl he cuts in half?

Devi: No.

"You should write a book titled *Sawless Magic* then," he said.

"And then I just fell apart?" What a great first line.

191

Brad couldn't shake the thought he'd done a disservice

to that uncomfortable couple on the train with his explanation of the world and Jackson Pollock. He never looked

me in the eye. She got hounded about shopping on their travel trips that night.

In the future, Brad could have said, Pretend the artist is your friend instead, until proven otherwise. You would never internally look at a work by a pal

and think, "I'm too stupid to figure it out." The AbExers were your friends.

The Impressionists too. They were out of the mainstream,

wanted to make art for people,

forget cathedrals built by monarchs. They were elevator doors sliding open, inviting you inside. Pollock as dancer, as Christ, as tack

thrower, as a philanderer, as spray bottle crusher. He knocked and knocked against the floor too. He commanded Hans Namuth to get out of the hole, "Come up here."

That was the depth he dug for. That was where he hid his bourbon. Jasper Johns on his hands and knees, pleading for pleasure. Rubbing palms all around

for a trap door latch. Frank O'Hara—*when I think of you in South Carolina,*

I think of your foot stuck in the sand.[144]

192

We were at the Clark Art Institute, and you said, Brad,

you need to see this. I had never come so close to gasping, looking at the John Singer Sargent meditation in white,

in light; looking at you looking at me. I already mentioned the postcards I bought, the allure of that woman, the resemblance to a porchlight.

I didn't remember until Higgs Beach today, the importance of the title, *Ambergris.*

This is how it always is with me, this knowing

---

[144] From the O'Hara poem "Dear Jap." Pull your foot out, see the hole. The world is pierced by Orpheus and friend.

something, sometimes for years, and then finding it. *Fumée d'ambre gris (Smoke of Ambergris)*

from 1880. *Smoke of Ambergris,* of course. Ambergris comes from the oil of the whale. Arrows

in the distance. Herman Melville nears the mountain's edge. Ambergris, from Clark Art Institute's website:

"The painting depicts a heavily draped woman inhaling the smoke of ambergris—

> a resinous substance found in tropical seawater and believed to come from whales.

It was thought in the Near East to be an aphrodisiac."[145]

193

With the sharpened pencil,[146] Brad bought in the gift shop of the MoCA he sat and drew; the trace of rivers connecting Lake McDonald through the Upper and Lower Flathead, around curved dots of towns, and down to Flathead Lake.

194

Brad's father always said:

---

[145] Steven Kern, excerpted from *The Clark: Selections from the Sterling and Francine Clark Art Institute*, Steven Kern et al. (New York: Hudson Hills Press, 1996), p. 116.

[146] Would you rather be the pencil in this world, or the pencil sharpener?

"Beauty is only skin deep. Ugly is to the bone."

195

Connect the dots and destinations. People, polka dots, and cells and atoms.

The couple on the train last night asked me to explain the work of Jackson Pollock. Afterward, I wished I'd mentioned World War 2.

On Facebook, there's a photo titled *Yellow Road*, a mass of autumn leaves covering the entrance streets to Glacier Park and leading to Lake McDonald.

Angela had asked, "You learned to drive in the university parking lot?"

The photo's comments say, *Yellow Brick Road.*
[COME HOME]

196

On the elliptical at the gym, I watch *Batman Begins*, with a video of him looking up. Closed Captions close on in, read: [water dripping] His baptism, looking up. His bats.

My lake. My *Frozen Lake*[147] (the first time Brad ever

---

[147] The *Buffalo Tom* song "Frozen Lake," on the album *Let Me Come Over,* 1992: "Give up my whole world /She's a translucent girl / In my

thought of that).

Anselm Kiefer looking up. Brad thought. I thought,
I thought; I thought about painting an elevator door
everywhere.

When the surface breaks from flailing or drips, hands
outstretched to grip unsteady realities—from the ripples stones or ashes cast, tears and tearing and below-view tremors—the concentric circles spreading outward
in departures, formerly reflected on the slimmest plane,
their tenuous reality recast from up above, shatters and
disappears.

In a letter to his wife back in Giverny, Claude Monet wrote:
"What a task this cathedral is!"

197

Opening a box of plastic straws; cities, all of them on I-95 where I got arrested; the Barbara Krueger LED signs scrolling words

---

frozen mind I'm lost in time / I take one more breath it's worse than death / Turn on all the lights alive with fright / See, she fits to me too easily / I, I'm borderline almost every time / Give up my whole world / She's a complicated girl / In my frozen mind I'm stuck in time / Give up my whole world / She's a complicated girl / In the frozen lake she comes and takes."

beneath the Hirshorn;

hot air balloons in sky (see Nadir, see the unlikelihood of that name); bowling pins from the setter's view, the ellipsis starting as your texting partners type; empty

space they used to occupy when fingers no longer insist; wine cellars; plastic water glass stackers the dishwashers

(men) lug to the dishwashers (machines) out back.

Stores for hubcaps and tire rim displays; the BEFORE moments when Millennium Falcon

starts to accelerate. Richard Serra's *Torqued Ellipses.*

How far away from a spot do you need to be to see it

as the world [AFTER], and how close you have to be to see a multiverse container in there? The estimates for galaxies keep increasing. How far away

do you need to get to see one spot contains a million-million other things?

How close do you need to get to understand a million things are one?

The meteor showers tonight. The meteor showers last week.

One light speck

in the Ben-Day sky revised by paintbrush stroke,

de Kooning at cocktail parties, partially drunk

and impartially having doubts. Sponge sides, foaming

pollution, the intrusion
of a matchstick to the dry fields of unsuspecting.

Bullets in boxes; bullet points; obnoxious comparison
crutches like apples to apples and dust to dust. Ashes;
my father's ashes sinking on Flathead Lake. Across the street
from my apartment at the Wilma, the sun strikes hard on water bends—reflects rock points and bottle
glass, resurfaces as resurrections—the sun revises sky.
Stand still; we'll build a raft of Kleenexes to hold to. Those tears
are epitaph. Jasper Johns exploding poet loves, and Lichtenstein borrowing your toothbrushes
the morning after. De Kooning had a downstairs doorbell system, you know. Depending
on how often you pressed the black nozzle of the button, his taste buds chose
licking or sandpaper, and he learned how much to love you. He blew bubbles made of TNT.

"Dynamite," he'd say, crushing words with absurd pronunciations. You lean, you sink,
he sends down the elevator to let you in.
Your windpipe, crushing.

198

When hypocritical Brad, always elsewhere,

found out Diaz had a book filled with footholds made
of footnotes, he thought: awful. He felt the same when he
heard Damian Farley Brighton[148] did this too.

However, Brad felt elated when an actor playing Damian
Farley Brighton told him, "Your story is inspiring."
The fact that Brad met both of these men
in Boston shows that every life, including his, had a
slight touch of Gump. He'd been
everywhere, met everyone.

Life is a series of extension cords. A cathedral
is an elevator ride.[149] A couple on the train; we ate in the

---

148 Brad was 98% sure he met Damian Farley Brighton (See blue bandana, see Alston, see alcoholism) before he relapsed, and before he killed himself, and before Brad knew he was literary royalty. Brad has forgiven his footnotes. Brad has not forgiven the world for ascribing his death to depression. He was an alcoholic. He was depressed. An alcoholic who does not take care of his sobriety first (he did not) and relapses (he did) and mixes that with a cocktail called depression (he did) is much more likely to commit suicide than anyone grappling with a single version of these things. The number one killer in America, anonymous and hidden from death certificates, called Heart Disease, Homicide, Suicide, Liver Disease, car accidents, natural causes, and undisclosed, is alcoholism. Calling Pollock's death a car crash, Rothko's death a suicide, or Damian Farley Brighton a victim of something besides alcoholism only confuses the world.

149 Brad's sponsor said to him when he was new: "Your alcoholism is progressive. It's like an elevator, but it only ever goes down. You can get off wherever you like, but if you get back on, it's only going further down." Brad was sure the guy was right, as his own disease was propelling toward inferno, something he only semi-understood when

dining car, white tablecloths

and steak. From Northern Virginia, they asked me to explain Jackson Pollock.

I closed my eyes and thought of Raymond Carver. I wondered if I were blind.[150]

199

The drawing remade the site of Brad's baptismal. The drawing remade the site

of his father's funeral too. The rivers were black and sharp and reflected back

like the curve in a woman's hair who drowns. Time is infinite, infinite

before and after, too.

My father always said:

"I've never had it so good."

---

the world came up and hit—jail cells, car crashes, busted relationships—and he sobered up a bit. Did Brad ever tell you he went to church and drank communion wine his last (I hope) day out there? That spiked vinegar blood probably saved his life from shaking loose his heart. A few months later he was in a church basement 12 Step meeting and realized it was the same room he had his last (I hope) drink in. A line from a favorite poem: *I keep thinking of "last" as final and "last" as most recent and wondering which is which.* ("Blue," by [REDACTED], *Hanging Loose*, Issue #84, 2004).

[150] See the story "Cathedral" from the collection of the same name, 1983.

200

Have you ever had the feeling of drowning? When and in what situation did this occur?

I have suffered from depression off and on practically my whole life. That feels like drowning in a tar pit. Sinking deeper and pulling harder every time you try to move. You can't even flail. I've also dreamed of drowning on the coast of New Hampshire. That water is so unforgiving and so inviting. I'd like to be the seaweed drifting in and out still anchored to the rocks, caressing the strands of seaweed next to it, in and out, softly, daily, nightly, sweetly, endlessly.

201

The last stanza of the poem *Trace* from September 30:

> Be quiet now and wait. It may be the ocean one,
> the one we want so to move into and become,
> it may be that one wants us out here
> on land a little longer
> going our sundry roads to the shore.

202

The last postcard you included is John Singer Sargent. We were in the gallery and you told me I had to look. *Smoke of*

Ambergris, from 1880.

I stunned myself. The white. *The white.* I stunned. I thought of Sargent in the Gardner Museum, music notes shown as men's heads tilting: singing.

I thought of Jack Spicer at the BPL, crying at the manuscripts of Emily Dickinson

in drunken mornings. I was shocked. Like when you walked me to your car, slightly ahead, and I took in every curve of you. Brad said something like "My phone still won't work,

so email me if you need me, tonight." Sitting idling in the drive for a moment; and you turned

on the porchlight.

See *Buffalo Tom*, "Porchlight." See your photo tangled on the ground. See the hood of light spilling from the woman in Sargent's painting.

I took out my sharpened pencil again and wrote and mailed it back to you.

203

Spicer's footnotes, Creeley's parentheticals, Alexie's fire

and booze, Olson

and the ocean, Martha Collins' colors: pinks and blue; black and white.

Kurt Vonnegut said, "Color was everything," in

Breakfast of Champions. Artists own the landscapes, maybe. But the poets own the punctuation and demanding truths. Artists own the land; poets own the landing.

How do you speak about yourself invisibly? When you get up that far and look, do you see the *Face of God?*

Tell me, she said, Whatever happened to your comic book collection?

Brad sold *Spiderman* and *Wolverine* for drugs; *X-Men, The Punisher.*

Of course, he regretted it when the plastic bags were empty.

204

It's a collage of sound, these notes, and music. Girls

in the gym are speaking

Eastern European. Brad never learned a language because it's nice not to understand

some things, like songs. I'm always astonished when people know the words. Like Newbury Street in Boston, and the melody of melting separating, distinct with found forms.

Like your love of Chamber Music, where things blend together. Like me and well-produced

rap music and collage. Curate with shock and awe, put two pictures there, together.

Brad walked the blocks and met Alyce on Newbury Street when

she rode down into town.

Of course, he fell in love with a girl who worked for the bus line Concord Coach.

By then, he feared all airplanes. He feared figures;
he feared the ground.

Brad's father always said:

"Break up with them right before Valentine's, Christmas, and their birthday.

If it's true love, they'll come back."

205

I said, you spent the weekend with the intellectual elite
in the Adirondacks on a lake making art, and I ate pancakes from dining hall plates, sat with murderers
and thieves. These worlds bridged lyrics
connect, may need a hurricane
translator to bind us. Multiverses are made of these stars, glitter of candles in eye shine, the residue of you
I keep carrying until we can pour out all our excesses
into the empty spaces of each other. Your lake;
your bottomless lake, and my brotherhood—each of us sipping
from the saucer, our horizon lines
are bent to full.

225

206

They call the court slips judges assign “gift certificates”
in The Keys. There's a reason
kilo got shortened to *key*, these networks of fishing nets and police chiefs shipping
weight so regularly; The Seven Mile Bridge required reinforcements. So I look down
at the break: A sticker on the back of the metal folding chair reads: *Adirondack.*
The first time my dad got sober, he started chewing pills to
relieve his back pain.
“Go to enough meetings in those unforgiving chairs, and you're
bound to get on the beans.” My friend Pat T would say: “What did I think about the speakers
with their uncomfortable shares; Hell, what do you think about my new Nike sneakers?
They’re Unstoppable Airs.”

Your host descends from the greatest American philosophers. My spiritual advisor
did 12 years for shooting a guy in the stomach,
dead. Years earlier, Mickey showed
for his first horse race reeking of booze. The trainer wouldn't
let him lead the pony out
to the starting gate. “Alcoholics aren’t like other people,” Mickey’d always say, “We celebrate

events before they get

to occur." "Also," he always says, "Kids fall in love.

Adults grow into love."

He was so short the gut shot was unintentional. But he definitely meant to kill

that guy. I patted his chest under a sweater some 40 years later and he thought I was checking for a heater, checking to see if he was packing.

Kenneth Koch in Brooks Brothers for years

before someone realized the store credit

card was the only form of currency Mr. Train had to dress himself with. A charge

account from his dad preserved that veteran in stripes from dressing post-War bohemian.

Where do we appear, and what light do we appear in?

If Kenneth hadn't showed at the door

the day after Frank died, Scarlett would be the only

O'Hara you'd ever heard of.[151]

---

[151]"Having a Coke With You" is an amazing love poem. Marge Gander once told me that O'Hara was sort of no good, that other than "Why I am not a Painter," what else was there? Everything I have hunted and pecked since has been a cover of long songs by Frank O'Hara titled "Ode to Willem de Kooning," "Meditations in an Emergency" and "Poem." "Poem," "Poem," and "Poem." When I die / and people are sad / tell them don't be sad / show up on my doorstep

207

River of tears; of sorrow. Veins and branches; roads. Telephone
wires, extension cords connect and stretch humanity.
Blackfoot River running through, as in the poem
"Salmon as Silver / Salmon as Fire:" The shards spread
out like ceremony. There were words
I am sure. There was opening and finding something
else / in there. And afterward,
this / nothing. Sun against shallows / sorting
its way out against the deepest parts.

My Montana father had requested his burnt-up ashes
scatter / on the skin of Flathead lake.

/ in Brooks Brothers clothes / a receipt for a pocket square / grab whatever you can find / from the Post-it notes on my kitchen cabinets / the journals I illegibly make love to with dyslexic eyes / the hackneyed hand of a man fighting back backwards / words he revived after dreaming / during road trips / and long lost love affairs / tell them these periods and question marks are the destinations / quotations / raise eyebrows and crease forehead lines / of friends / parenthetical frowns and smiles / the joys of texts in nights as dark as vowels / flicked off / and moaned / he was looking / for this / I was looking at him / to look for this / turn and walk away / humming a song you've never heard / and check your boots / those first boots you crossed in a January classroom / see the treads filled up with glass and sand / look down again / look up / the elevator doors are open / I'll meet you there someday.

All of us are finding our way home. All of us are returning. /

All of us are becoming

something else, washing off this residue / of road, one silver-

stained and salmon

orange season at a time.[152]

208

Dear Angela:

I'm aware you don't like beautiful men. I'm not sure if that's a red flag. Or a non-issue. I heard what you said about long-distance poets; I heard

what I said about dating. I am aware of the strangeness of this sentence and have debated telling you over the past couple of days for various

reasons, including my respect for you, for our relationship, for miles of distance and logistics; for the fact I would never have planned or guessed saying this: Tuesday night was the best date I've had in years.

I did not think it was a date. I did not plan it as such. You may not have had the same response. But it's how I felt after. It surprised me in a way. It also seemed perfectly obvious in a way.

I'm not sure what to do about that besides tell you. And

---

[152] First published in *Sourland Mountain Review,* October 2016, by the author.

tell you if you felt similarly, let's do it again sooner rather than later.

209

River of *Moby Dick* ropes. What we strike with arrows, catch, and hold, may swamp us and then turn around and

drown us too. In the aftercare counseling Brad attended after detox, before the same woman sent him over to the shrink, she said,

"What do you know about denial?"

"It ain't just a river in Egypt," he said and smiled. She didn't

laugh. Her eyes got wide like saucer plates.

210

Doing the elevator meditation one morning, Brad saw God

on the beach. His feet pressed in the sand on the way to greet the light. Later, he arrived at the South Beach,

Miami 12 Step meeting and there was a sign on the wall: Everything is Under Construction. The topic for discussion was

a reading from the Thought for the Day book: Pain is the touchstone of all spiritual progress.

Brad glanced down. All around his chair, there was sand

spilled everywhere in piles.

211

Devi: I'm flailing in and out of the groove like a drunk Madonna.

Brad: Working on Brad's "Ben Day Dots of Grass" a few days back I realized the movie *Desperately Seeking Susan* (soundtrack source of said groove named *Groove*) is my baseline foundation

for what NYC is like. I've been listening too, to New Found Glory's remake of *Crazy For You* a lot, like a drunk and confused

Basquiat (PS he and Madonna had relations).

212

Later, after she told me she was suicidal, she sent me a photograph of a butterfly posed on a window. She wrote *#mykindredspirit #trapped*

Brad: But so close to a window opening at any moment

Devi: *That shit is locked and inaccessible*

Brad: Not if you focus on helping the butterfly. Then let the universe take care of you

Devi: *Brad.*

213

My counselor told me to stand with my hand out,
stand still,
and let the butterfly land.

[Lichtenstein was lamenting the conformity, confinement,
and trappings of tract housing, assembly-line automobiles,
and mass-produced culture with his identical
and repetitive dots]

The night after you apologized, I woke from a dream
on a mind-beach with God
I handed him a gold pocket watch and then
I looked down and saw shattered shards
sticking up from piles and piles of hourglass sand.

214

[In the *Monet/Lichtenstein Rouen Cathedrals* exhibition at the Museum of Fine Arts in Boston in 2011, there was a sense of intimacy between the two artists, a conversation, and a reverence to contemplate. These works propel the viewer back toward the originals, rather than remain in consideration of

Lichtenstein. They create distraction rather than limits]

Angela: So you like the constraint
of the form, then? Brad's smile began
to expand and fill in all around. He knew then
they'd name her Dorothy.[153]

215

Break the windows
and fly.
The elevator's on
its way.

[153] Dot.

BIOGRAPHY

A graduate of the Creative Writing Program at the University of Montana, Kurt Cole Eidsvig's work in both poetry and art criticism has been featured in regular columns for Big Red & Shiny, ArtsAmerica, SpinRecords, and Examiner.com. He has been featured and published in outlets like *The Boston Globe, Slipstream, Hanging Loose, Borderlands, Main Street Rag, Poets Reading the News, The Improper Bostonian,* and *The Southeast Review.* Eidsvig has taught art and writing at UMASS Boston, the University of Montana, and the Isabella Stewart Gardner Museum, and he worked as a gallery assistant for the Arts on the Point Sculpture Park in Boston. Kurt has won a Massachusetts Cultural Council Fellowship, a Warhol Foundation/ Creative Capital Award, and the Edmund Freeman Award. In addition to DROWNING GIRL, he is the author of the books ART OFFICIAL (Terror House Press, 2023), OXYCONTIN FOR BREAKFAST (Main Street Rag, 2023), and POP X POETRY (KCEMCS, 2021). With deep Boston and Montana roots, he lives and works in Key West, Florida, and maintains a website at www.EidsvigArt.com.

ABOUT THE PRESS

Unsolicited Press is based out of Portland, Oregon and focuses on the works of the unsung and underrepresented. As a womxn-owned, all-volunteer small publisher that doesn't worry about profits as much as championing exceptional literature, we have the privilege of partnering with authors skirting the fringes of the lit world. We've worked with emerging and award-winning authors such as Shann Ray, Amy Shimshon-Santo, Brook Bhagat, Kris Amos, and John W. Bateman.

Learn more at unsolicitedpress.com. Find us on twitter and instagram.

www.ingramcontent.com/pod-product-compliance
Lightning Source LLC
Chambersburg PA
CBHW021717120626
46545CB00004B/1606

* 9 7 8 1 9 6 3 1 1 5 1 0 9 *